Write for
First Certificate

✓ ⊘ HW   10.1 / 10.2a / 10.3a

next wesday — Wister test

HW   wesday   p.38

Write for First Certificate

Elizabeth and Paul Cane

Edward Arnold
A division of Hodder & Stoughton
LONDON MELBOURNE AUCKLAND

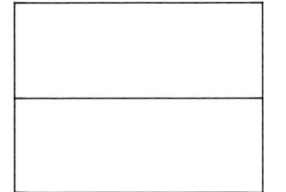

Acknowledgements

The authors would like to thank Roger Gower for his help and encouragement and for some ideas on punctuation, Gillie Cunningham for a couple of her brilliant ideas, and their colleagues and students in Cambridge for help with trialling material and for providing compositions.

The authors and publishers would like to thank the following for permission to reproduce photographs illustrations and text:

Barnaby's Picture Library, The Bell School, Cambridge, Julia Dall, Falcon Holidays, International Music Publications, Taurus Graphics, Pantek Arts, Neil Phillips.

© 1990 Elizabeth Cane and Paul Cane

First published in Great Britain 1990

British Library Cataloguing in Publication Data

Cane, Elizabeth
Write for first certificate.
1. English language. Composition – Questions & answers – For non-English speaking students
I. Title II. Cane, Paul
808'.042'076

ISBN 0-340-50030-1

All rights reserved. No part of this publication may be reproduced or transmitted in any form or by any means, electronically or mechanically, including photocopying, recording or any information storage or retrieval system, without either prior permission in writing from the publisher or a licence permitting restricted copying. In the United Kingdom such licences are issued by the Copyright Licensing Agency: 33-34 Alfred Place, London WC1E 7DP.

Typeset in 10/11 pt Rockwell by TecSet
Printed and bound in Great Britain for Edward Arnold,
the educational, academic and medical publishing division of
Hodder and Stoughton Limited, Mill Road, Dunton Green,
Sevenoaks, Kent by Thomson Litho Ltd, East Kilbride, Scotland.

Contents

	Page
Acknowledgements	iv
Plan of the book	vi
Introduction	viii
Unit 1 Opinions	1
Unit 2 Informal letters	11
Unit 3 Narratives	20
Unit 4 Speeches and instructions	30
Unit 5 Formal letters	39
Unit 6 Descriptions	49
Unit 7 Advantages and disadvantages	59
Unit 8 Reviews	68
Unit 9 Checking and correcting compositions	77

UNIT	TOPICS	PLANNING AND GUIDED WRITING OF COMPLETE COMPOSITIONS	PLANNING AND GUIDED WRITING OF PARAGRAPHS
1 Opinions	Men and women; drugs	Overall organisation – completing a plan Building up from ideas to plan to completed composition	'Key' sentences – opening sentences in a paragraph
2 Informal letters	Letters; people you write to	Overall organisation Letter layout Paragraph ordering Replying to a letter	'Key' sentences – opening and concluding sentences Putting sentences into the correct order
3 Narratives	Accidents; misfortune	Overall organisation Writing a text from given words and pictures	Introductory paragraphs Putting sentences into the correct order
4 Speeches and instructions	People in groups; a wedding	Overall organisation – completing a plan	Completing a paragraph using a picture and given words
5 Formal letters	Job applications; a language school in England	Overall organisation Letter layout Writing a letter from a given plan	Completing a paragraph from given words and phrases
6 Descriptions	Countries; stereotypes	Overall organisation Writing a text from a given picture and plan	Building a paragraph from given vocabulary around a topic
7 Advantages and disadvantages	Transport; prison	Overall organisation – completing a 'spider' plan Building up from ideas to plan to completed composition	Matching examples to main points Concluding and introductory paragraphs
8 Reviews (including set book compositions)	Books; reviews	Overall organisation – completing a plan Building up a text from a plan and given information	Using 'referring' words within a paragraph
9 Checking and correcting compositions	Assessing and improving compositions; correcting errors – focus on spelling; a letter, narrative and discursive composition		

INTRODUCTION vii

STYLE AND FORMALITY	PUNCTUATION	CONNECTING WORDS	ADDITIONAL AREAS OF LANGUAGE	PAGE
Keeping to the point	Introduction to the most common punctuation marks	Words used to develop an argument – *furthermore, another point...,*etc	Giving opinions	1
Informal letter style	Punctuating a letter	Common informal connecting words	Asking for things Making suggestions Giving advice	11
Getting hold of the readers' attention Using a variety of words in place of *say* and *tell*	Punctuation of direct speech	Words used to link events in time – *while, eventually,* etc	Past perfect and past simple tenses	20
Identifying the tone and atmosphere Formal and informal introductions and conclusions	Full stops and commas	Words used to sequence instructions – *next, then,* etc. Revision of time words	Prepositions of place	30
Formal letter style contrasted with informal	Capital letters	Words used to contrast ideas – *although, despite,* etc.	Making complaints Salutations and valedictions Introductory and concluding sentences	39
Factual and expressive styles Using paragraphing for clarity and emphasis	Apostrophes	Words used to express attitude – *naturally, unfortunately,* etc	Vocabulary used to describe impressions	49
Cutting out repetition of single words	Semicolon (contrasted with full stops and commas)	Revision of words introduced in Units 1 and 5	Making one side of an argument weaker	59
Being clear and concise – cutting out repetition of ideas	Extension and revision of use of full stops and commas	Words used to link reasons and results – *therefore, due to,* etc.	Using inversion	68
				77

Introduction
For students and teachers

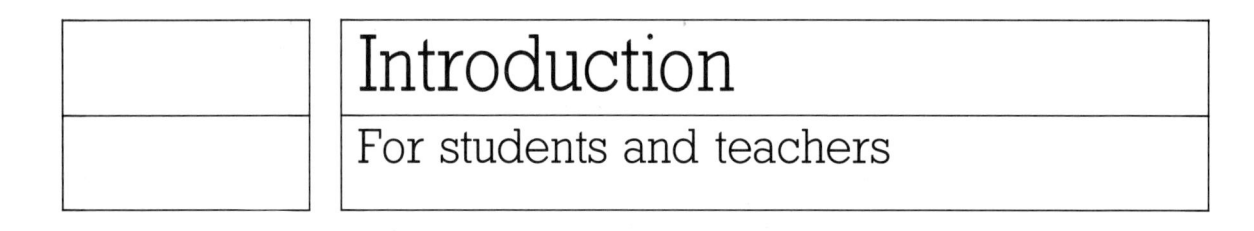

How to use Write for First Certificate

What does the book cover?

Units 1–8 give practice of the composition types tested in the Cambridge First Certificate in English (FCE) examination – letters, narratives etc. Unit 9 helps students to improve on the first draft of a composition by identifying and correcting mistakes.

A key is available giving answers to the exercises in Units 1–8, and corrected versions and suggested marks for the student compositions in Unit 9.

Who is the book useful for?

The book has been written for people taking the Cambridge First Certificate examination. However, it will also be of use to any learner of English at an intermediate or upper intermediate level who needs to produce the types of writing that are covered in this book.

Can the book be used by a student working on his/her own?

Yes. Individual students can work through all the activities except the discussion and pairwork exercises, checking their answers in the *Key* as they go along. However, they will need a teacher to give them individual feedback on their compositions

Does the book only involve writing?

No. There are many reading passages which are aimed at getting the students to analyse different aspects of writing in interesting ways. There are discussion and pairwork activities which provide variety and useful speaking practice, as well as helping the students towards the general aim of a better understanding and use of the skills necessary for effective writing.

One of the most important characteristics of the book is the setting of tasks so that the students can work out 'rules' for *themselves* – rather than merely being told them. In the same way, the students are guided towards a clearer understanding of the process of writing that best suits them. Therefore it is useful if students can work together and discuss (in pairs or small groups) as many of the activities as the teacher thinks best.

INTRODUCTION ix

Is it necessary to work through every activity of every unit?

No, although complete coverage of the composition types that occur in the Cambridge First Certificate examination will only be achieved by going through the whole book. If time is short or it is felt that the students need to work on a limited number of composition types, then the teacher and/or the students can choose to do the units they need most. Furthermore, a class could leave out different parts within a unit that they felt they already had a good understanding of.

The units are not entirely independent of each other: for example, the punctuation and connectors work is built up and revised as the book goes along, and the second unit on letters revises and takes parts of the first unit further. Therefore it is better, but not absolutely essential, to keep to the order of the units in this book.

How do I work through a typical unit?

All of Units 1–8 have three parts:

Part 1: Planning

A 'Focus on the topic' activity is designed to get students in pairs or groups sharing their ideas on a topic before they read about it. Then one or two examples of the relevant composition type are read by the students. They are guided towards an understanding of how to plan their own work by analysing the overall organisation of the examples. The students' attention is focused on the general subject of each paragraph and the ordering of paragraphs; how to arrange sentences *within* a paragraph is left until later.

Part 1 usually finishes with further oral exploitation of the topic or a reference to a composition title later in the unit which allows students to explore the topic in writing.

Students should be encouraged to work together on the speaking activities and to compare their answers during the reading and writing tasks.

Part 2: Practice of language points

Part 2 consists of four or five (usually separate) exercises that aim to get the students analysing and then practising an area of language that usually has particular relevance to the composition type focused on by that unit.

Most of the exercises have two parts: the first leads the student to a greater awareness of the area of language under study and the second is a productive practice activity. As with the activities in Part 1, students will benefit from working together and helping each other towards more accurate use of the language items.

The areas that the exercises cover are:

- Punctuation: the uses of the most common punctuation marks are introduced, practised and in some cases revised.
- Connecting words: these are grouped according to use. The more unfamiliar ones are introduced as well as practised.
- Style and formality: a variety of exercise types that enable the students to look at their written work more critically at the first draft and

editing stages so as to develop a greater understanding and more effective use of style and register.
- Grammar, vocabulary and functions: items are chosen only if they have obvious use in a particular composition type. For example: past perfect and past simple tenses for narratives, the function of giving opinions for opinion compositions and vocabulary associated with impressions and feelings for descriptive writing.

Part 3: Guided writing

The final part of the unit gives direct written practice of the areas looked at in Part 1 and some of those in Part 2. It is hoped that the students will use most of the items of language they have worked on in Part 2, even if their use is not demanded explicitly.

Part 3 is usually made up as follows:

- A short text or paragraph building activity: this aims at improving the skills of paragraph construction and also giving practice of the exercise types found in the last part of Paper 3 of the First Certificate examination.
- The writing of a complete composition: students are asked to work together on the ideas and planning stages of the composition. It is suggested that the actual writing is done individually at home. These compositions can be brought to class and edited/improved by other students if there is time, and finally given to the teacher for checking. Alternatively the students can work in small groups in class, each group producing one composition; groups can then exchange compositions and suggest improvements. This editing of each others' work should make students better at checking and revising their own work.
- Exam practice: students are given five typical First Certificate composition titles to choose from, to be done in the same time and to the same length as in the exam. All the compositions are of the type focused on in the unit. The students can do as many of these compositions as they and the teacher feel appropriate.

Unit 9

This unit gives students the opportunity to assess and correct three compositions: a letter, narrative and discursive composition. There is also a section on common spelling rules.

Students could do Unit 9 after finishing the other units or work through the correction of the letter having finished Unit 2, the narrative after Unit 3 and the discursive composition after Unit 7.

Cambridge First Certificate – the Composition Paper

What does the Cambridge First Certificate Composition Paper include?

You must choose to answer any two of the five questions in the composition paper. Your two compositions, each between 120 and 180 words, must be written in one and a half hours. The first four questions together offer a choice of four composition types. These nearly always include a letter, a discursive/opinion composition and a narrative. The narrative and letter often include descriptive writing and sometimes there is a separate descriptive composition. Frequently a speech is included. Question 5 offers you a choice of three titles – one on each of the set texts. These texts are usually novels, plays and short stories. You can only write a composition on one of them. Obviously you will have to read one or all of the books to be able to answer question 5. However, it is not obligatory to answer the set texts question.

What is the examiner looking for?

The examiner will be assessing how well you organise your composition as a whole and will also want to see if you can use paragraphing appropriately and whether your sentences and ideas are well organised within the paragraphs. Accuracy and appropriateness of spelling, vocabulary, grammar and punctuation are very important. For a good grade you will also have to show that you can use a reasonably wide range of these areas of language.

What happens if I write too little or too much?

If you write less than 120 words, the examiner will adjust the maximum mark. For example, a three-quarter length answer deserves three-quarters of the mark that it would have been given. If you write much more than 180 words, the examiner will draw a line at the approximate place where the correct length is and assess what comes before this. However, credit may be given for relevant material appearing later.

Are there any guidelines I can follow?

- Always read the question most carefully.
- Make sure your composition covers only what the question asks.
- Plan your composition concentrating on the meaning of what you are going to say; at the very least your plan should contain notes on the main idea(s) of each paragraph.
- Don't write less than 120 or more than 180 words.
- When you have finished, check your composition for:
  meaning – are your ideas relevant, clear and well organised?
  mistakes – is your use of grammar, vocabulary, spelling and punctuation as accurate as you can make it?
- If you are not sure of the accuracy of a particular word or phrase, then write it in another way that you are sure is correct.

Opinions

You will practise:
- planning and organising 'opinion' compositions
- using the most common punctuation marks
- giving opinions
- using connecting words to develop an argument
- style – keeping to the point
- completing a text from notes and prompts

Part 1 Planning

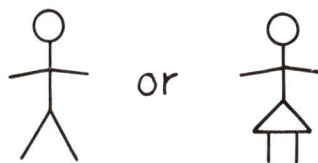

Focus on the topic

Imagine that you had the chance to live your life again. Would you prefer to be a man or a woman? Some English teachers were asked this question and some of their answers are listed below.

– Choose a word for each space: 'woman', 'women', 'man' or 'men'.
– All the teachers gave reasons for their opinions. Discuss which reasons you agree, half agree or disagree with.

'A _woman_ because they are the ones who have the chance to work for the future of the world by bringing up children in a loving environment.'

'A _man_ because they are the ones who take the important decisions in life. Most world leaders and famous historical figures have been _men_.'

'A _woman_ because they are nicer people! It's nearly always _men_ who start wars or commit horrible crimes.'

'A _man_ because I'd hate to actually have a baby and do all the boring work that _women_ usually do.'

'A _man_ because they lead more interesting lives and have more freedom.'

'A _woman_ because I'm fed up with going out to work and I'd like to sit at home and put my feet up most of the day!'

2 OPINIONS

A. We asked Jane Bolt, an ex-teacher, to write down her ideas on this topic. Read what she wrote and answer the questions below.

① Of course it is difficult to say whether I'd prefer to be a man or a woman if I had a second life because, as a woman, I cannot say that I know exactly what it's like to be a man. However, my experience of life – including twenty years of marriage and the bringing up of two sons – would lead me to choose to be a man in a second life for two main reasons.

② First of all, across the world, women suffer from repression by men. Throughout history men have made women feel that they are inferior. This means that women don't have the same confidence as men and this leads them to let men decide important things at the family level and also in terms of how society is organised. This is clear from the fact that at a national level nearly all top politicians are men. How many Russian and American presidents have been women?

③ Secondly, women do not enjoy the same opportunities as men in the world of work as it is extremely difficult for them to escape from the prison of housework and child care. One could argue that this is another example of men repressing women but I am dealing with work separately as it is so important to me personally. When I got married I had a more interesting and better paid job than my husband. However, because of pressure from him and my parents I gave up work and since then have had to concentrate on bringing up *our* children and doing necessary but incredibly boring housework. Personally, I have found this work very frustrating; I feel that I would have developed more as a human being and contributed more to our marriage if I had been able to continue with my career.

④ To sum up, I feel sure that I would lead a more complete life if I could take advantage of the greater opportunities that men have. Being a man in a second life would also allow me to persuade men that women should have greater control over their own lives and over society itself!

OPINIONS 3

1. Choose the best **two** descriptions of this composition.
   It gives:

   (a) the main advantages of being a woman and disadvantages of being a man.
   (b) the main advantages of being a man and disadvantages of being a woman.
   (c) the main advantages and disadvantages of being a woman and also those of being a man.
   (d) the personal opinion of the writer.
   (e) the personal opinion of the writer *and* the other side of the argument.

2. Read the writer's rough plan for the composition.

   > Paragraph 1: prefer to be a _man_ for two main reasons
   > Paragraph 2: first _reason_ (point) — men, women and (i) _man_
   > Paragraph 3: second _reason_ (point) — men, women and (ii) _opinion_
   > Paragraph 4: my being a _man_ — chance to change the attitudes of _men_ towards _women_ !

   (a) Choose a suitable word for each underlined space (_____).
   (b) In paragraphs 2 and 3 the first sentence is the important 'key sentence'. Choose one word from the 'key sentence' of paragraph 2 to complete (i). Choose one word from the 'key sentence' in paragraph 3 to complete (ii).

   Note: 'Key sentences' often tell you the subject of the whole paragraph.

B. 'Opinion' compositions often have a structure like this:
   First paragraph: Introduction
   Middle paragraph(s): Explanation
   Final paragraph: Conclusion

1. Here are three groups of ideas for things to include in each of the main parts of an 'opinion' composition. Match each group with the part of the composition (introduction, explanation or conclusion) that it gives ideas for.
   Group 1:
   (a) your opinion – but don't repeat anything you've already said
   (b) a more amusing, light-hearted point
   (c) looking at the subject in the future

4 OPINIONS

Group 2:
(a) your interest in the subject
(b) your *general* opinion about the subject
(c) an historical overview of the subject
(d) why this subject is important

Group 3:
the reasons for your opinion: reasons that are not obviously connected usually go into different paragraphs

2 (a) Which one of the 'ideas for things to include in an introduction' (see above) did Jane Bolt make the most important part of her introduction?
   (b) Which sentence in her conclusion restates her general opinion in a different way from her introduction?

C. 1 (a) Imagine that you had the chance to live your life again. Would you prefer to be a man or a woman? Answer this question yourself and make notes of the most important reasons.
   (b) Discuss your opinions, giving reasons, with three or four other students.

2 Listen to the preference, with its single most important reason, of each student in the class. Which is the most common preference and what are the most popular reasons?

There is a composition on this subject at the end of the unit.

Part 2 Practice of language points

A.1
Punctuation – the use of the most common punctuation marks

Match each punctuation mark with its name and the sentence that describes how it is usually used. Then decide if it is followed by a capital letter to start a new sentence or not.

(Remember that a sentence is a group of words, including a subject and a verb, that is grammatically independent and can stand alone.)

The first one has been done for you.

OPINIONS 5

Symbol	name	use: It's used....
?	Apostrophe (1)	to finish a sentence that expresses strong feeling (5) Capital letter
,	Speech marks (2)	when you want to join two grammatically independent sentences because their meanings are closely connected (8) not
;	Full stop (3)	to finish a question – followed by a capital letter
" "	comma (4)	to surround the exact words said by someone (2) not
.	Exclamation mark (6)	to allow a pause within a sentence when reading *or* to separate all the different parts of a list *except* the last two (4)
	Question mark (7)	to point out where a letter is missing *or* to show the possession of something by someone (1)
!	Semicolon (8)	to finish a sentence (3) Capital letter

2 Rewrite the following sentences using a different punctuation mark to complete each one. Each underlined space needs one punctuation mark.
  (a) I don'_t really want Brian'_s book.
  (b) "_I know what I want,"_ he whispered.
  (c) It's going to be cold today, isn't it?_
  (d) Three times four equals twelve._
  (e) She's a very good tennis player;_ it's her squash that isn't so good.
  (f) That's fantastic!_
  (g) I'll go shopping,_ call in at Jim's,_ pick up the baby and then go home.

B.1 Connecting words used to develop an argument

Look at the list of connecting words and phrases and decide which ones do **not** fit naturally into the space in the short extract below. Explain why.

Furthermore,   However,   What is more,   Another point is that
Moreover,   But,   On the other hand,   Firstly.

How good is eating out in Britain?
Well, many tourists complain about the quality of cooking in some British restaurants. _____ it's difficult to find cheap places to eat and drink that stay open later at night. One person I spoke to said that...

2 Read the paragraph below which argues for the setting up of a discothèque. Put 'Firstly', 'Furthermore' and 'Another point is that' once each in the most appropriate places places to separate the different points that support the writer's opinion.

6 OPINIONS

In my opinion firstly there is no doubt that a good disco would greatly benefit our town. It would give our young people something to do in the evenings. At present there is a lack of facilities for teenagers, excepting of course our well-equipped sports centre. More tourists could be persuaded to stay the night if we could provide lively evening entertainment in the form of a good disco. Indeed, one of the most common complaints we hear in the tourist office is that visitors would like a wider choice of things to do in the evening. A disco would of course provide work for some of the unemployed; this and the other points I have mentioned would improve both the welfare and the prosperity of the town.

C. Phrases used to give opinions

Change the sentences *on a paper* using the words given in brackets, but keep the meaning the same. Leave out any unnecessary words. The first sentence has been done for you.

(a) I think murderers should be executed. (opinion)
   Answer: In my opinion murderers should be executed.
(b) I believe that criminals need help. (point of view)
(c) I feel that this new technology is more trouble than it's worth. (seems)
(d) I'm of the opinion that Jones should get the job. (consider)
(e) I think space exploration is a complete waste of money. (mind)
(f) There's no doubt that he's lying. (sure)

D.1 Style – keeping to the point

Read the title and the first paragraph of the argument below against smoking and decide why the writer has decided to leave out the words in brackets.

2 Read the rest of the argument and complete these sentences.
   (a) Paragraph 2 is about the dangers of passive smoking for _____.
   (b) Paragraph 3 is about the dangers of passive smoking for _____.

3 Now improve paragraphs 2 and 3 by leaving out two sentences from each.

Smokers Are Killing Us!

Evidence in a recent report from the Independent Scientific Committee on Smoking and Health about the effects of cigarette smoking on non-smokers shows that *all* of us are in danger. (And soon the price of cigarettes will be going up.) There is now no doubt that if you work, live or come into regular contact with people who smoke, then there is a strong possibility of your health being adversely affected.

   The report indicates that babies of fathers who smoke are likely to be smaller and weaker than babies of non-smoking fathers. Of course it is already well known that pregnant women who smoke can damage the health of their babies. My sister smoked twenty cigarettes a day when she was expecting her first child. Another worrying point is that smoking just *before* the start of the pregnancy can affect the baby later. I heard recently that certain foods may harm unborn babies.

OPINIONS 7

The report goes on to say that if you don't smoke but live with or come into regular contact with smokers, then your chances of getting lung cancer increase by between 10 and 30 per cent. Unborn babies are definitely at risk if their parents smoke. These figures suggest that in Britain there are between 100 and 200 deaths of non-smokers every year as a result of passive smoking. Despite the great number of deaths due to cancer each year, medical researchers are still no nearer to finding a cure for this terrible disease. The major conclusions that we must draw from all these statistics are that the health of *everyone* is put at risk by smoking and that smokers should give up.

4   Smoking probably causes more deaths than any illegal drug. Should young people be stopped from smoking or just discouraged? How? Discuss.

Part 3 Guided Writing

A. Text completion

Read the extracts taken from conversations about the possible building of a new motorway through an attractive part of the countryside.
Complete the letter below arguing **against** the motorway, using all the points in the extracts. For each point write **at least one other sentence** explaining it or giving an example of it.

8 OPINIONS

> ① "the/a motorway would be a great danger to local wildlife, particularly the deer..."
>
> ② "The children will need to cross it to get to school..." such a not a road ~~it~~ would
>
> ③ "...noise and other forms of pollution..." first/third
>
> ① ④ "...destroy our lovely valley, the most beautiful for miles around..." last or second

---

Dear Sir/Madam,

Having lived in one of the villages in the Trent Valley for over twenty years, I am writing to complain about the proposed siting of the new motorway. My wish to have the motorway built elsewhere is based on four main reasons.

① First of all,... it would

② What is more,...

③ Another point is that the local resident would suffer from noise.

Finally, and perhaps most important of all,...

Hoping that these points will persuade you to change the proposed plans.

Yours faithfully,

B. From the title to the completed composition

You are going to write a composition entitled *either*:
  'Why the drinking of alcohol should be made illegal.' *or*
  'Why the drinking of alcohol should not be made illegal.'

1 Discuss:
   (a) What are the laws about alcohol in your country? Think about age of drinkers, where alcohol can be drunk and alcohol and driving.
   (b) What (other) drugs are legal? Tobacco? Marijuana? Uncontrolled used of 'medical' drugs?
   (c) Are some of the legal drugs stronger or more dangerous than some of the illegal ones?

off the point = irrelevant

OPINIONS 9

10 OPINIONS

(a) With two or three other students make two lists of reasons
   (i) why alcohol should be made illegal.
   (ii) why alcohol should not be made illegal.

You may want to consider these points:
- violence
- social traditions
- acceptance by some religions
- prohibition by some religions
- deaths on the road
- cost
- personal freedom to choose
- makes you relaxed, sociable
- health

(b) Discuss in your group which list contains the strongest reasons.

3 Working individually, choose the composition title from the two at the beginning of this question that you want to write about. Your composition should be less than 180 words, so you should explain your opinion without giving the other side of the argument.
   Follow the outline plan below; look at Part 1, Section B for ideas on the introduction and conclusion.

Paragraph 1: Introduction.
Paragraph 2: Two or three connected reasons, with explanation/ examples if necessary.
Paragraph 3: Two or three connected reasons, with explanation/ examples if necessary.
Paragraph 4: Conclusion.

C. Exam practice

Choose any of these titles and write a composition of between 120 and 180 words. Each composition should take no more than 45 minutes.

(a) What can we do to prevent the increase in starvation in poorer parts of the world?
(b) Why is pop music so popular among young people and sometimes very unpopular with parents?
(c) Argue for *or* against the banning of smoking in public places.
(d) If money were no problem, what ways would you choose to learn English as quickly as possible? Give reasons.
(e) Would you choose to come back as a man or a woman if you had the chance to live a second life? Give reasons.

INFORMAL LETTERS 11

Informal letters

You will practise:
- organising the layout (addresses, date etc.) correctly
- planning and organising informal letters
- linking ideas using punctuation and suitable connecting words
- making requests, suggestions and giving advice
- writing individual paragraphs
- putting paragraphs into the best order

Part 1 Planning and layout

Focus on the topic
- Think of some people that you might write informal letters to.
- Think of the subject of an informal letter to someone at work and the subject of a formal letter to the same person.
- Is the person you are writing to or the subject of the letter more important in helping you decide whether your letter will be formal or informal?

12 INFORMAL LETTERS

A. Read the letter and answer the questions below.

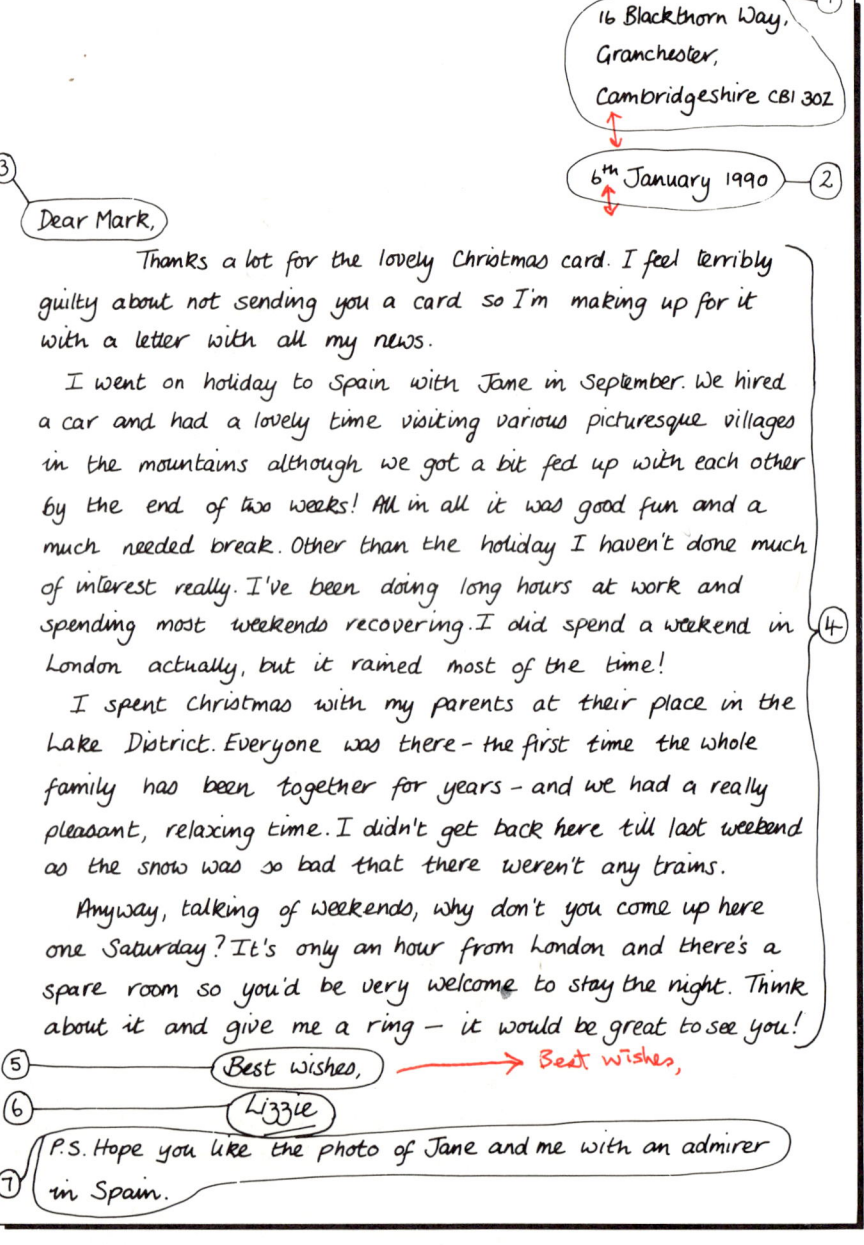

1 Imagine that this letter was written as a First Certificate composition. Complete the instructions for writing the composition.

'Write a letter...'

INFORMAL LETTERS 13

2 Match each numbered part of the letter with the sentence below which best describes it.

(a) The valediction (closing phrase) 5
(b) The sender's address: 1
    house number and street,
    village/town/city,
    county (if this is not clear already) and postcode
(c) The salutation (opening phrase) 3
(d) The postscript (if you want to put something at the end that you forgot to mention earlier) 7
after → (e) The date 2
(f) The writer's signature 6
(g) The body of the letter 4

3 Are these statements true or false?   → shine

(a) The writer and receiver are girlfriend and boyfriend. F / Best wishes + 1st para
(b) The writer lives in the county of Granchester. F   Town
(c) It would be acceptable for Lizzie to write her name above her address. F
(d) It would be wrong to write 'love' instead of 'best wishes'. F
(e) 'Dear Mark' could also go a little further to the right on the same line. F
(f) It doesn't matter if 'Best wishes, (Lizzie)' isn't in the middle of the line. T

4 These are headings for each of the paragraphs in the letter. Match each heading with the paragraph it describes. The first one has been done for you.

(a) Important things Lizzie has been doing – Paragraph 2
(b) Looking forward to seeing Mark Paragraph 4
(c) Why she's writing Para 1
(d) A family get-together Para 3

B. Informal letters usually have three main parts:

First paragraph: introduction A
Middle paragraph(s): main contents B
Final paragraph: conclusion C

Here are three groups of ideas for things to include in each of the main parts of an informal letter. Match each group with the part of the letter (introduction, main contents or conclusion) that it gives ideas for.

Group 1
last →
(a) looking forward to some contact with the reader in the future C
(b) making a warm, more personal comment about the reader C
(c) giving an excuse for finishing the letter C

Group 2
first →
(a) thanking reader for letter, card, present etc. A
(b) apologising for not writing earlier A

14 INFORMAL LETTERS

(c) giving reasons for writing
(d) giving general idea of rest of letter

Group 3

(a) describing what you've been doing recently
(b) giving/asking for information, advice etc.

C. The sentences below are typical ways of expressing some of the ideas given in Section B. However, the words have been mixed up. Put the words back into the correct order and then match each sentence with one of the ideas in Section B.

Example: really I I'm recently in sorry been contact haven't.
Answer: I'm really sorry I haven't been in contact recently. (Group 2(b) – an idea for the introduction.)

(a) next seeing you I'm forward weekend really to looking.
(b) I present enough sent the thank can't you lovely for you.
(c) where think you me carpet tell you you beautiful that could Do bought?
(d) directions new I'm to to house writing you give our.
(e) I'll now catch post stop can the so I.

Part 2 Practice of language points

A. Punctuation and layout

Re-write this letter, setting it out correctly, putting it into three paragraphs and including all necessary punctuation. The body of the letter should contain five sentences.

13 peter street great burton yorkshire yk2 6sp 16th december 1989 dear robert just a quick note to tell you a little about marys cottage its about ten miles south of manchester so take the main road to macclesfield for nearly ten miles and then turn sharp left under a railway bridge follow this road for another mile and youll see the house on the left at the first junction its no 13 and its got a green gate unfortunately i wont be able to join you there but have a great time anyway and ill hope to see you in a month or so love john

I look forward to hearing / meeting from you. (Formal).

INFORMAL LETTERS 15

B. Connecting words

Fill in the blanks choosing the best answer.

> 16 Higham Hall,
> Leeds University,
> Leeds LR5 4GH
>
> October 5th *Year.*
>
> Dear Mum and Dad, — *informal.*
>   (1) *Well*, here I am at last, a university student sitting at my desk trying to do some work! (2) *As* you can see, I'm not *really* working but have decided to write you a brief letter telling you how I'm getting on instead! (3) *Actually* I've done quite a lot of work already; can you imagine, I haven't (4) *even* missed a lecture yet!
>   On the first evening after you'd gone and I'd unpacked my things, I decided to go down to the college bar (5) *to* have a drink. (6) *Just* as I was leaving my room the student in the room next to mine opened his door, (7) *So* we introduced ourselves and went for a drink together. His name's Arthur and he seems very nice.
>   This morning I got up early (8) *So as not to* miss breakfast. (9) *However*, unfortunately college breakfasts are not all that they could be; I think I'll make my own in future! I had my first lectures this afternoon which, I must say, were (10) *really* very interesting.
>   (11) *Anyway*, I *really* must get down to some work now, so I'll stop here and write to you again at the weekend. Make sure you give my love to everyone at home.
>
>   Love John
>
> P.S. (12) *By the way*, I think I've left my diary at home, so could you send it if you find it? Ta!

beginning of the sentence → (9)

1 (a) Hello (b) Well (c) First
2 (a) So (b) As (c) If
3 (a) And (b) Actually (c) Hopefully   = in fact.
4 (a) already (b) really (c) even
5 (a) for (b) to (c) then
6 (a) Just (b) Really (c) Although
7 (a) after (b) but (c) so
8 (a) so as not to (b) not (c) but
9 (a) However (b) Although (c) And
10 (a) quite (b) really (c) also
11 (a) Also (b) What's more (c) Anyway
12 (a) In fact (b) By the way (c) However

16 INFORMAL LETTERS

C. Asking for things

Complete the sentences keeping the meaning as near as possible to the starred (*) sentence. Only change parts of the starred sentence if you have to.

* Could you send me my cheque book? *

Example: Could I ask you ....?
Answer: Could I ask you to send me my cheque book?

(a) Would you mind *sending me my cheque book* ?
(b) I wonder *if you would send me my c. book* ? [Conditional]
(c) Do you think *you could send me my c. book* ?
(d) You *couldn't send me my c. book* , could you?
(e) Can *you send me my c. book, please* ?

D. Making suggestions and giving advice

Put the verbs in brackets into either the gerund ('-ing' form), or the infinitive with or without 'to'.

(a) How about (go) *going* to the theatre while you're here?
(b) You'd better not (do) *do* that.
(c) She really ought (see) *to see* a doctor.
(d) I'd advise you (take) *to take* the car to a garage.
(e) Why don't you (see) *see* if Alex is doing anything tonight?
(f) I should (speak) *speak* to the office manager about it if I were you.
(g) I'd definitely recommend (have) *to have* a good rest and a break from work. [you to have.]
(h) Have you thought of (try) *trying* a camping holiday?

Which five sentences are *stronger* (advice), and which three are *weaker* (suggestions)?

strong b, c, d, f, g | weak a, e, h

Part 3 Guided writing

A.1 Building a paragraph

Put these sentences into the correct order so that they make a single paragraph. The paragraph is taken from a letter to a friend from someone who is on holiday in Egypt. The first sentence has been done for you.

> Dear Jonathan,
> I'm writing just to prove that I really am in Egypt! Although I'm not actually writing this half way up one of them, I can see the pyramids from the café where I'm sitting.
> We've been in Cairo for nearly a week now, and it really is the most incredible place...

INFORMAL LETTERS 17

5 (a) As well as the architecture, there's the River Nile of course.
3 (b) First of all it's got the most fantastic range of historical buildings.
6 (c) This gives the city a bit of quiet and calm, even if you've got to hire a boat to find it!
4 (d) However, a lot of these old places are in a very ☆ bad state of repair.
7 (e) Most of all, though, it's the liveliness of the people and the non-stop activity that <u>makes the place so memorable</u>.
1 (f) We've been in Cairo for nearly a week now, and it really is the most <u>incredible place</u>.
2 (g) Everything from pyramids to railway stations!

b + g.

Which sentence (the key sentence) tells the reader the general idea of the whole paragraph?

INFORMAL LETTERS

2 This letter is to a close friend. Write suitable opening and closing sentences for the second paragraph, making sure the opening sentence introduces the general idea of the whole paragraph. Then compare your sentences with other students'.

> Dear Rosemary,
>   Thanks a lot for your letter, which I got the other day. It was great to hear from you and keep up to date with your latest news, both good and not so good. *......I was very sorry to hear about your uncle's illness.........* I know what this kind of illness is like as a cousin of mine had it a year or two ago — you may remember. In fact she made a full recovery and is even thinking of going back to work. Is your uncle in hospital or being looked after at home? I'd like to write to him so could you give me his address if he's anywhere other than at home? *Anyway, do keep in touch if there is anything I can do.*
>   On a happier note, I'm hoping to have a party some time next month, so ....

B.1 Putting paragraphs into the correct order

Put the paragraphs of this letter into the correct order.

> Firs House,
> Haddenham Road,
> Victoria 3206,
> Australia
>
> 7 January 1990
>
> My dear Kim,
> (a) However, it isn't all sun, sea and sand in Australia. I actually do have to do a bit of work sometimes! Joking apart, the facilities at the hospital are excellent and the other nurses are very friendly. You don't have to do quite so many hours a week here but I would say that the relations between doctors and nurses are better in Britain. Perhaps it's a bit unfair to say that as I suppose I haven't really been here long enough yet.
> (b) I thought I'd drop you a line now that I've been here for just about a month. What with finding somewhere to live and starting a new job, life has been incredibly full, so I'll restrict myself to the main impressions the place has made on me and the big differences I've noticed between Britain and Australia.
> (c) Well, I must get back to the beach I suppose! Sorry, I won't mention it again. Please DO write soon as I'd love to hear how all our friends at the hospital are getting on. What have you been doing since I left? Anything exciting? Don't forget to send my regards to everyone and, as I said, I'm expecting you any time.

INFORMAL LETTERS

(d) I found myself a flat in three days. That's another thing — accommodation is much easier to find. So you're very welcome to come out and stay at any time as long as you give me a bit of warning. I know the flight's expensive, but you really *must* make the effort. I know you'd have a great time as there are so many interesting things to do: it really would be the chance of a lifetime.

(e) Well, first things first — yes, you guessed it — the weather! I hear it's snowing in London; here the sun shines most of the day, I go swimming in the sea every weekend and you wouldn't believe the suntan I've got! I think the weather and the fact that everyone seems so relaxed over here are the two most obvious differences.

Best wishes (from the sunny side of the world), Peter

2 Imagine that you are Kim Hardy and that you recently received the above letter. You used to work with Peter as a nurse until he emigrated to Australia. Reply to his letter, not forgetting to set out your address and the date correctly.

C. Exam practice

Choose any of these titles and write a composition of between 120 and 180 words. Each composition should take no more than 45 minutes.

(a) Write a letter to your parents asking if you can bring a friend home for the weekend. Tell them about this friend.
(b) You are on holiday, staying with some friends of your parents. Unfortunately you are not enjoying yourself, so write to a friend telling him/her about it.
(c) You are working at the London branch of your company for a short period. Write to an elderly relation back in your home country describing your experiences.
(d) You were on the way to a friend's party when you had a minor car accident and had to go to the police station. Write to him/her to apologise and explain what happened.
(e) Write to your girl/boyfriend saying that you want to end your relationship and explaining why.

Narratives

You will practise:
- planning and organising narratives
- introductory paragraphs
- punctuation of direct speech
- using different reporting verbs
- past perfect and past simple verb forms
- writing narratives from notes and pictures

Part 1 Planning

Focus on the topic
- Can you think of any famous plane crashes?
- Have there been any in your country?
- Describe to another student an accident (of any kind) that you have had in your life.

 A. Read this extract from a book about a famous plane crash in the Andes mountains in South America. The introduction has been left out. Answer the questions below.

> For eight days the Chileans, Argentinians, and Uruguayans searched for the plane. Among the passengers there had been not just the fifteen members of the rugby team but twenty-five of their friends and relations, all coming from prominent families in Uruguay. The search was fruitless. The pilot had evidently miscalculated his position and flown north towards Santiago when he was still in the middle of the mountains. It was early spring in the southern hemisphere, and the Andes had suffered exceptionally heavy falls of snow. The roof of the plane was white. There was little chance that it would ever be found, and less chance still that any of the forty-five passengers and crew could have survived the crash.
>   Ten weeks later a Chilean peasant tending his cattle in a remote valley deep in the Andes saw, on the far side of a mountain torrent, the figures of two men. They made wild gestures and fell to their knees as though in supplication, but the peasant, thinking that they might be terrorists or tourists, went away. When he returned to the same spot the next day the two figures were still there, and once again they made signs to him to approach. He went to the bank of the river and threw a piece of paper and a pen wrapped in a handkerchief to the other side. The bearded, bedraggled figure who received it wrote on the paper and threw it back to the peasant. It read: 'I come from a plane that fell in the mountains. I am Uruguayan....' (adapted from 'Alive!' by Piers Paul Read)

NARRATIVES 21

There were sixteen survivors. It was only later that the world would learn of, and be astounded by, the faith and friendship which inspired them, and the suffering which forced them to eat the bodies of their dead friends in order to stay alive.

1   (a) What words come to your mind when you read this story? (e.g. *touching* 'horrifying', 'sympathy'). Think of as many words as you can to describe your feelings.
    (b) How would you feel and what would you do if you were in this situation? Discuss.

2   (a) Write a title for the story. *Survived from the Hell*.
    (b) Read the story again and decide what the subject is of the two main paragraphs. *The search / Getting out*

B. *HJ* Read these possible introductions to the story and a reader's comments about them.

1   Match the introductions with the comments which best describe them.

   Introductions:
   1 On October 12th, 1972, a plane carrying a Uruguayan amateur rugby team was crossing the Andes on its way to Santiago in Chile. Most of the passengers were young. Some were laughing and joking together and *d* others were looking out of the windows trying to catch a glimpse of the mountains through the clouds. There was a holiday atmosphere on board – some of the boys were even throwing a rugby ball up and down the passenger cabin. Suddenly the plane went into a dive from which it never recovered.

   2 On October 12th, 1972, a Fairchild F-227 carrying a Uruguayan amateur rugby team set off for Santiago in Chile – a destination the plane was *a* never to reach. The events which occurred in the following weeks make up a story which has made a deep and lasting impression on me.

   3 On October 12th, 1972, a plane carrying a Uruguayan amateur rugby team crashed high up in the Andes. Some survived the crash but were forced eventually to eat the flesh of their companions due to lack of food. *c* After several weeks two young men managed to find their way out of the mountains and bring about the rescue of those left at the plane.

   4 It has been said that it often takes great suffering to bring out the best qualities in men and women. The companionship and courage which war *b* seems to create is a case in point. The story of the survivors of the plane crash in the Andes in 1972 is another example.

   Comments
   (a) 'I like this one – just enough background information and then a very personal comment.'
   (b) 'Interesting – a general observation about hardship that leads naturally into the Andes crash.'
   (c) 'I don't really like this one – perhaps it tells us too many of the important stages of the story too early so that we don't really need to read the other paragraphs.'

22 NARRATIVES

(d) 'Great – good "setting of the scene" clearly describes the atmosphere just before the crash. The last sentence is very dramatic and encourages us to read further.'

2   Do you agree with the comments? Which introduction do you like best? Discuss.

C. Short narratives often have a structure like this:

First paragraph: introduction
Middle paragraph(s): main contents
Final paragraph: conclusion

1   Here are three groups of ideas for things to include in each of the main parts of a narrative. Match each group with the part of the narrative (introduction, main contents or conclusion) that it gives ideas for.

Group 1
(a) giving background information – describing relevant events that happened before your story starts.
(b) 'setting the scene' – describing the situation/people/feelings at the point where the story begins.
(c) giving the readers an exciting 'taste' of the story to catch their interest – without telling them too much!
(d) making a general point (of which your story is a clear example).

Group 2
(a) a dramatic part of the story (often the end) which you want to keep as an exciting climax.
(b) consequences of the story – effects it has had on you, people involved in it or even the whole world!
(c) a short personal evaluation of the story, e.g. 'In conclusion I can honestly say that I have never had a more frightening experience in all my life.'

Group 3
developing the story – describing what happened.

2   Look back to the two main paragraphs of the Andes story. One paragraph describes what happened in one half of the story; the other includes background information as well. Which is which?

3   Which two 'ideas for things to include in a conclusion' (see section C1 above) are used in the conclusion to the Andes story?

4   In pairs, retell the story in your own words with one student telling the first part and the other the second.

Part 2 Practice of language points

A. Punctuation of direct speech

1 Look at these sentences, noting when and where commas (,) and speech marks ('...') are used.
  Question and exclamation marks (? !) are followed by capital letters – except sometimes in direct speech. Check when (see sentences (d) and (e)).
  Why do (d) and (e) *not* have a comma at the end of the direct speech?
  (a) 'The train leaves at 5.00,' said Greg. → verb of reporting
  (b) 'If you do that again,' Peter said, 'then I'll break every bone in your body.'
  (c) 'This food is horrible,' she said. 'I can't eat it.'
  (d) 'Look out!' she said.
  (e) 'What's the time?' he said.

2 Rewrite the following sentences with the correct punctuation.
  (a) Have you got a room with a bath she asked
  (b) I'll do it tomorrow John said
  (c) You should see your doctor said Ann which one do you go to
  (d) help he said
  (e) stand up he said and listen to me

B. Style

It would be better to use a wider range of reporting verbs (instead of 'said') in the exercises above on punctuation.

1 Replace said in each of the sentences in section A1, (a)–(e), with the most suitable of the following reporting verbs, using each verb only once:
  shouted   remarked   complained   asked   threatened
     d   a   c   e   b
  Example (question 1(a)): 'The train leaves at 5.00,' remarked Greg.

2 Now do the same for the sentences in section A2, (a)–(e), using these reporting verbs:
  promised   ordered   enquired   cried   suggested
    b   e   a   d   c

C. Connecting words used in narratives

Read the following story and choose the best linking word.

Looking back I knew it had been too easy. A hotel had been booked, the car had been delivered and we'd set off at dawn with the sun rising over the sleeping city. We were off to visit Palmyra, an ancient city in the Syrian desert. The four of us all shared the excitement that an adventure into the unknown brings. (1) _Little_ did we know what was to come.
  (2) _Having_ travelled for an hour we were enjoying the scenery when the car began making strange noises and (3) _then_ spluttered to a halt. We tried unsuccessfully to start it. (4) _Eventually_ we got a lift to the nearest village. There we tried to find a taxi to take us to Palmyra. This proved difficult until an old man (5) _finally_ understood and went off. He returned later with his taxi which looked as old as Palmyra! (6) _After_ agreeing on a price we got in and waited. And waited. What we didn't know was that the 'taxi'

24 NARRATIVES

wouldn't leave until it was full. Hours later we actually left with the old car laden with four other paying passengers. We had hardly gone five kilometres (7) _when_ we arrived in another village. Everyone got out except us as we knew it couldn't be Palmyra. However, after a long conversation we realised that our taxi driver had brought us to a village with a similar name to Palmyra. What's more he refused to take us any further. So out we got and sat in the village square feeling furious.

(8) _Just_ then a bus came along with Palmyra written on the front. Much relieved we jumped on and although we had to stand we didn't care. Despite the squash and heat the hours passed by. (9) _As_ we got off the bus the wonderful sight of the graceful ruins lifted our spirits and the day's events were forgotten. We'd arrived (10) _at last_.

1 (a) Little (b) How (c) Nor
2 (a) While (b) Having (c) We
3 (a) after (b) next (c) then
4 (a) Lastly (b) Eventually (c) At the end
5 (a) even (b) finally (c) next
6 (a) After (b) As (c) Before
7 (a) then (b) after (c) when
8 (a) At this moment (b) Just (c) Immediately
9 (a) As (b) After that (c) While
10 (a) lastly (b) at last (c) at the end

D. Using past perfect and past simple verbs to describe past events

Look at these sentences describing parts of the story above. They have been put on 'timelines' to show which events happened first.

The events marked (1) happened **before** those marked (2).

(a) 'When dawn came we had already had a large breakfast.'

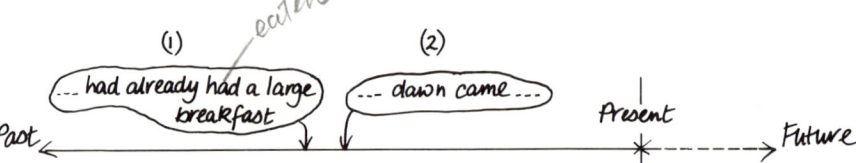

(b) 'After our car had broken down we got a lift to a nearby village.'

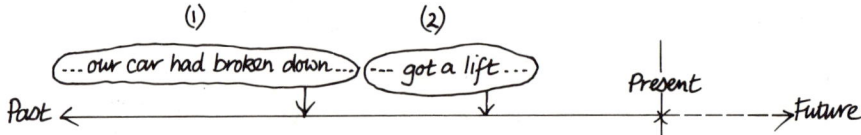

NARRATIVES

(c) 'No sooner had we arrived than we all felt much happier.'

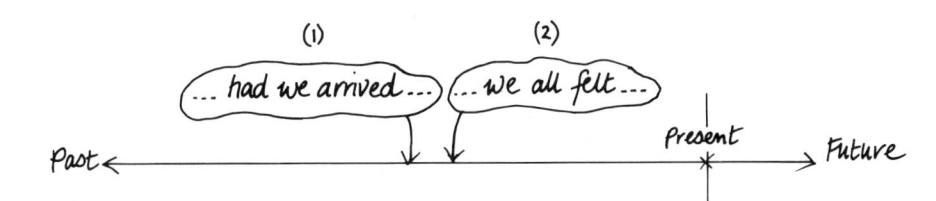

We often use the past perfect (had + past participle, e.g. had taken) to show when one event happened before another in the past.

Words such as 'after', 'when', and 'as soon as' are also used to link past actions.

1. Put these three sentences on 'timelines' in a similar way to the examples above.
   (a) My train had already left when I arrived at the station.
   (b) Tim found out that someone had stolen his car.
   (c) Man had tried to fly long before aeroplanes were invented.

2. Join each pair of sentences to make one sentence using the words in brackets. Use the past perfect once in every answer to emphasise that one event happened before the other. Make any other changes that are necessary.

Example: The phone rang. I got into the bath just before that. (... hardly ... when ...)
Answer: I had hardly got into the bath when the phone rang.

(a) I listened to the news. I immediately telephoned my mother.
   (As soon as ...)
(b) I saw Henry. Later I went to the theatre.
   (... after ...)
(c) It started to rain. I finished the gardening only a minute before that.
   (... just ... when ...)
(d) They finished painting the kitchen. So I then put the furniture back in.
   (... because ...)
(e) I sat down to my dinner. The next moment the door bell rang.
   (... hardly ... when ...)
(f) I taught in Spain for a year. Before that I was in Egypt.
   (... after ...)
(g) I got to the accident. The police arrived before me.
   (When ... already ...)
(h) The price of oil went up. It immediately went down again.
   (No sooner ... than ...)

26 NARRATIVES

Part 3 Guided writing

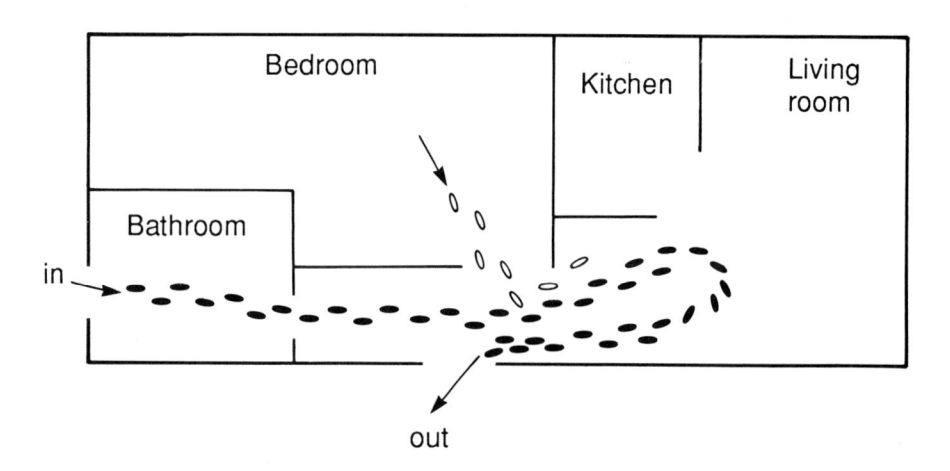

A. Putting sentences into the correct order

These sentences make up a complete story about a burglary but have been put in the wrong order. Work with a partner to put the sentences into the correct order, using the plan of Sheila's flat to help you. The first sentence has been marked for you.

(a) The burglar continued through into the living room and Sheila had to decide whether to keep quiet or do something more positive.

(b) As he obviously wasn't going to leave just because he'd been told to, she decided to confront him face to face.

(c) One night my sister Sheila, who lived alone at the time, was fast asleep dreaming about some friends coming to visit. (1)

(d) The girl stared at her fearfully for a moment and then was gone in a mad rush past Sheila and out through the main door.

(e) I don't think Sheila ever slept well in that flat again, and in fact she soon moved out to share with a friend.

(f) At first she wasn't sure if this was part of her dream or not.

(g) She walked from the bedroom through to the living room and turned on the light.

(h) However, this noise was followed by the distinct sound of soft footsteps in the hall and she knew she wasn't dreaming; there was a burglar in the flat!

(i) His response to this call was to go silent and stop whatever he was doing.

(j) Suddenly she was woken by a noise coming from the bathroom.

(k) She decided on the second option: 'I know you're in there – now get out!' she shouted.

(l) There, to her amazement, Sheila was faced by a young girl of about twelve who was even more frightened than she was.

There is a composition on this subject at the end of the unit.

NARRATIVES 27

B.1 Writing a story from pictures and notes

In pairs describe to each other what happened in the picture story below. Try **not** to use the notes.

28 NARRATIVES

PICTURE 1
One day — I — three year old cousin — zoo. Set off — happy — excited. Arrived — many animals — begin — Bird House.

PICTURE 2
I — parrots. I not notice Alex — monkeys. Cold — woolly hat — dummy. Loud cry. I saw — chimpanzee — Alex's hat and dummy.

PICTURE 3
Crowd amused — sight — Alex — started crying.

PICTURE 4
Zookeeper arrived — suggested — into cage — hat and dummy back. Bonzer — banana — zookeeper — hat. Bonzer — allowed — keep dummy.

PICTURE 5
Left — Alex — hated dummy — never — dummy — since. Funniest — life.

2 Write a story of about 200 words based on the pictures, finishing with the words '... one of the funniest days in my life.' Use the notes to help you and include some ideas of your own.

The pictures are in the correct order but you must decide where the paragraph breaks must be. Three or four paragraphs in all should be enough.

C. Exam practice

Choose any of the these titles and write a composition of between 120 and 180 words. Each composition should take no more than 45 minutes.

(a) You were asleep one night upstairs in bed when you were woken up by the sound of footsteps downstairs. Tell the story of what happened after this.
(b) Write a composition ending 'Suddenly I heard an alarm clock ringing and I realised that what had happened before had only been a dream!'
(c) You had a car accident yesterday that was partly your fault. Describe in detail the events that led up to it, the accident itself and what occurred afterwards.
(d) You were very poor until you unexpectedly inherited millions of pounds from a long-lost relative a few years ago. Describe what you did with the money and how your life changed.
(e) Write a composition about either a very boring or very exciting day in your life.

UNIT 4 Speeches and instructions

You will practise:
- planning and organising speeches and instructions
- punctuation – commas and full stops
- connecting words used to sequence instructions
- prepositions of place
- recognising formality in speeches
- writing from notes

Part 1 Planning

Focus on the topic

Think back to the last time you heard or gave a speech and describe
- where you were
- the people speaking and those listening
- what the speaker said
- why you did or didn't enjoy the speech

A. Read this speech and answer the questions below

A big welcome, everyone, from all of us at the Bond School on this the first day of your course. We hope you'll enjoy your time in England and learn a lot of English at the same time. I'm Mary Greeble, the Principal of the school, and I'm going to tell you which rooms to go to and then we'll give you a short test to get an idea of your level.

If you open your folders the first thing you'll see is a plan of the school. Has everyone found it? I'll give you directions to your rooms and we can use that as a chance to practise your listening and get used to doing everything in English. So see if you can follow my instructions and find your way to your rooms yourselves. But – of course – if you're not sure where to go, do ask! Right; we are in the Assembly Hall which is the large room at the top of the plan on the right – it's marked with a cross. Those of you specialising in English for Business should go to Room 4. Go out of this room through the small area for hanging coats and turn right into the corridor. Go straight along the corridor and down a few steps into the lobby between the Main and New buildings. Go through the door on your left into the New building and then into Room 4 which is the second room on the right.

If you are doing the English Literature option, go out into the corridor in the same way but follow it in the opposite direction. Walk past some stairs on your left and you will see Room 9, your classroom, immediately in front of you just where the corridor turns right. If you get lost, please don't be afraid to ask for help! Remember that Business is in Room 4 and Literature in Room 9.

SPEECHES AND INSTRUCTIONS 31

I'll leave you now to go to your classrooms and will see you later today to tell you more about your course and the school. So the best of luck with your studies and I'm sure that your stay in England will be both enjoyable and rewarding.

1 Decide where Rooms 4 and 9 are on the plan of the school.

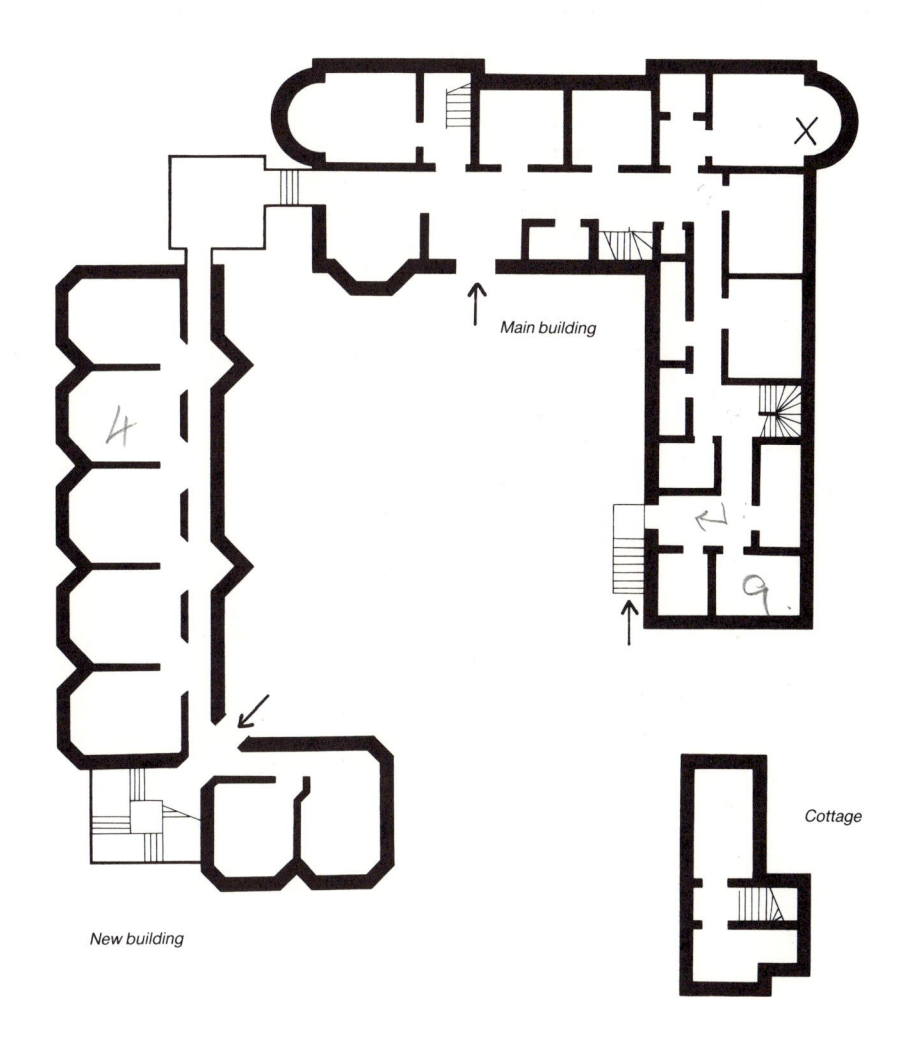

Main building

Cottage

New building

2 (a) Who is giving the speech? Principal
(b) Who are the people listening? students
(c) Has the speaker met these people before? No she hasnot
(d) Is the speech very formal, semi-formal or very informal? formal, semi
(e) Which is the best description of the atmosphere of the speech?
  – tense, nervous
  – amusing, 'jokey'
  – warm and relaxed but serious ✓

32 SPEECHES AND INSTRUCTIONS

B. Complete Mary Greeble's notes describing the purpose of each part of the speech. Put one word only in each space; the first letter of the first word has been put in.

(a) We<u>lcome</u> the students, *introduce* myself and tell them the <u>reason</u> for doing the test.
(b) Tell the <u>English</u> for *business* students where their *classroom* is.
(c) Tell the English *literature* students where *their classroom* is.
(d) Say that I'll <u>see</u> the students later; <u>wish</u> them luck.

C. Speeches often have a structure like this: *purpose*

First paragraph: introduction
Middle paragraph(s): main contents
Final paragraph: conclusion

Here are three groups of ideas for things to include in each of the main parts of a speech. Match each group with the part of the speech (introduction, main contents or conclusion) that it gives ideas for.

Group 1
main contents giving the information, instructions etc. that you want the listeners to know

Group 2
Conclusion
(a) something amusing
(b) saying how much you hope the listeners will enjoy themselves
(c) looking forward to talking to the listeners at another time

Group 3
introduction
(a) asking for quiet or the attention of the listeners
(b) welcoming the listeners
(c) introducing yourself
(d) giving the main purpose of your speech

In the introduction and conclusion to her speech Mary used all the ideas in Groups 2 and 3 except two. What were the two ideas she did not use?

(a) — group 2
(a) — group 3

Part 2 Practice of language points

Punctuation – full stops and commas

A.1 Which of these sentences (if any) have incorrect punctuation?
(a) Kate went to the cinema on Sunday afternoon. After that she had a game of tennis.
(b) Kate went to the cinema on Sunday afternoon, after that she had a game of tennis.
(c) Kate went to the cinema on Sunday afternoon and after that she had a game of tennis.

SPEECHES AND INSTRUCTIONS **33**

2 Rewrite these instructions putting a full stop, a comma or no punctuation at all where you see the dots (...). Don't forget to use a capital letter after a full stop.

A Nice Cup Of Tea, English Style!

(a) Boil the water ... after you've filled the kettle.
(b) When the water is hot ... use a little of it to warm the teapot ... before putting the tea leaves in.
(c) Pour the boiling water on top of the tea leaves ... after that you need to let it brew for five minutes.
(d) While it's brewing ... put a little milk in the cups ... adding sugar if you want.
(e) Finally ... the tea having brewed ... pour it into the cups ... don't forget to drink it!

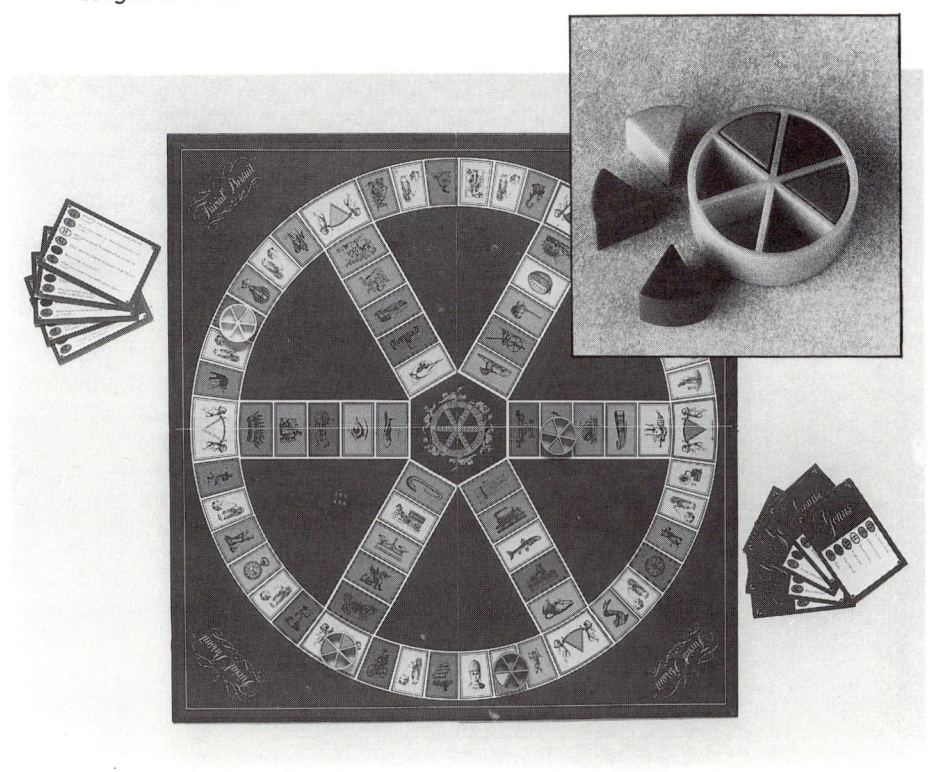

B. Connecting words used to sequence instructions

Bob is explaining the game Trivial Pursuit to Pam. Complete the dialogue by choosing the most appropriate connecting words.

Pam: So, how do you play this game, Trivial Pursuit?
Bob: OK. Let's see. (1) _____ you get a token and six differently coloured wedges which fit inside it – the token I mean.
Pam: What do you do with them?
Bob: Well, all the players start at the centre of the board with their empty tokens.

34 SPEECHES AND INSTRUCTIONS

Pam: Why empty?
Bob: You can only put a wedge in your token (2) _____ you've answered certain questions correctly. The idea is to move round the board filling your token with wedges.
Pam: OK. So we start in the centre. What's the _____ thing you do?
Bob: The first player rolls the dice and moves their token according to the number on the dice – in any direction.
Pam: I see; so if you get a '3' you move three spaces.
Bob: Exactly. Now (4) _____ moved three spaces, say, another player will ask you a question from the cards in the question boxes.
Pam: What type of question?
Bob: Well, it depends on the colour of the space you're on. A yellow space means a history question, a brown one indicates literature and so on.
Pam: And I suppose you keep rolling the dice and moving your token (5) _____ you get a question wrong.
Bob: Yes. (6) _____ the next player takes their turn.
Pam: Right. I see that six spaces have wedges drawn on them. Suppose you land on one of these – what do you do (7) _____?
Bob: If you land on one of those and answer the question correctly, you can place a wedge in your token. For example, if you land on a blue wedge space and answer correctly you put a blue wedge in your token.
Pam: So (8) _____ you try to move to the other wedge spaces?
Bob: That's it. (9) _____ your token is completely filled, you must make your way back to the centre of the board.
Pam: What do you do (10) _____ you've got back there?
Bob: The other players choose a question type which they think will be difficult for you and then ask you one of these questions.
Pam: And you hope to get it right! Only (11) _then_ do you win the game, right?
Bob: You've got the idea. Want to have a game?
Pam: Why not!

1 (a) First of all (b) When (c) Before
2 (a) at the moment (b) while (c) when
3 (a) next (b) later (c) last
4 (a) having (b) I (c) when — _after you have_
5 (a) when (b) until (c) while
6 (a) After (b) Later (c) At that point
7 (a) then (b) after (c) at this time
8 (a) later (b) once (c) after that
9 (a) Then (b) As soon as (c) Before that
10 (a) once (b) while (c) during — _immediately after_
11 (a) after (b) then (c) when

SPEECHES AND INSTRUCTIONS **35**

C. Prepositions of place used in instructions

~~Done~~

This exercise gives instructions for drawing a picture of geometric shapes. Look at the picture and complete the instructions below by putting a preposition in each space. The first one has been done for you.

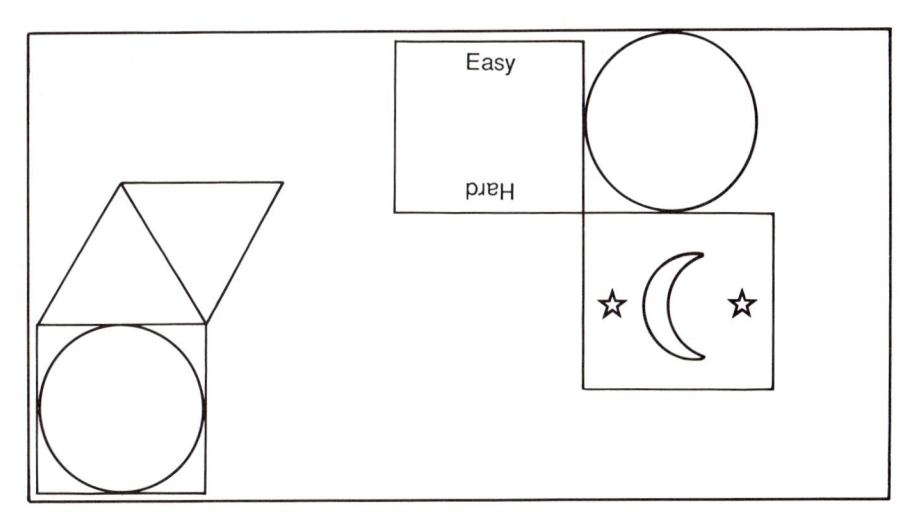

Draw a square (1) __in__ the bottom left hand corner of the frame. (2) __Inside__ the square there is a circle. Draw a triangle (3) __on__ top (4) __of__ the square, and then another triangle touching the top right side (5) __of__ the first triangle. Now put a square (6) __in__ the middle (7) __of__ the frame, (8) __At__ the top. (9) __Inside__ this square write 'easy' (10) __at__ the top and 'hard' (11) __at__ the bottom – but write 'hard' (12) __upside__ down. Next (13) __to__ the same square, (14) __to__ its right, draw a circle. Immediately (15) __under__ this circle draw another square, touching the circle (16) __at__ one point. Finally, inside this last square draw two stars with the moon (17) __between__ them.

2 In pairs, draw a different picture of geometric shapes. Do not show your picture to your partner.
   One student describes his/her picture and the other student listens and draws, asking questions to check understanding if necessary. When you have finished, compare the two pictures – they should be the same!
   Now repeat the activity, but this time the second student gives instructions and the other one draws.

D. Style – formality

hw

Which **three** of the following examples would you expect to be the most informal? Discuss your reasons.

A speech or talk given by:
(a) a student to the rest of your class about a holiday in the United States. *Informal*
(b) the Director to a large number of the employees about the work of a woman who is retiring after twenty years with the company. *Formal*
(c) the manager of a football team to his players about the match they have just played. *Informal*

36 SPEECHES AND INSTRUCTIONS

they know each other quite well

Informal (d) a man to some of his close friends who have organised a surprise birthday party for him.

Formal (e) the head of a university to the final year students and their parents at the graduation ceremony when the students receive their degrees.

2 Decide if each of these sentences from speeches is
   – formal or informal
   – more likely to be from the beginning or the end of a speech.

Formal / end (a) I don't wish to keep you any longer but I would like to say, once again, how truly grateful we are for your marvellous work.

Formal / begin (b) Ladies and gentlemen, please allow me to interrupt you so that I can say a few words about the happy couple.

Informal / begin (c) Excuse me everyone, but could we have a bit of quiet, please?

Informal / end (d) Anyway, I'm sure you've heard enough of me by now so I'll finish off with a little something about Harry that should make you laugh.

Formal / end. (e) May I conclude by asking you to raise your glasses and drink to the future happiness of Ted and Pam?

Part 3 Guided writing

A. Giving directions

Your friend George is getting married on Sunday and has left a note telling you how to get to his parents' house on the morning of the wedding.

Make all the changes and additions necessary to produce the seven complete sentences which make up George's note. Note carefully from the example (a) what kind of alterations need to be made. Use the map to help you.

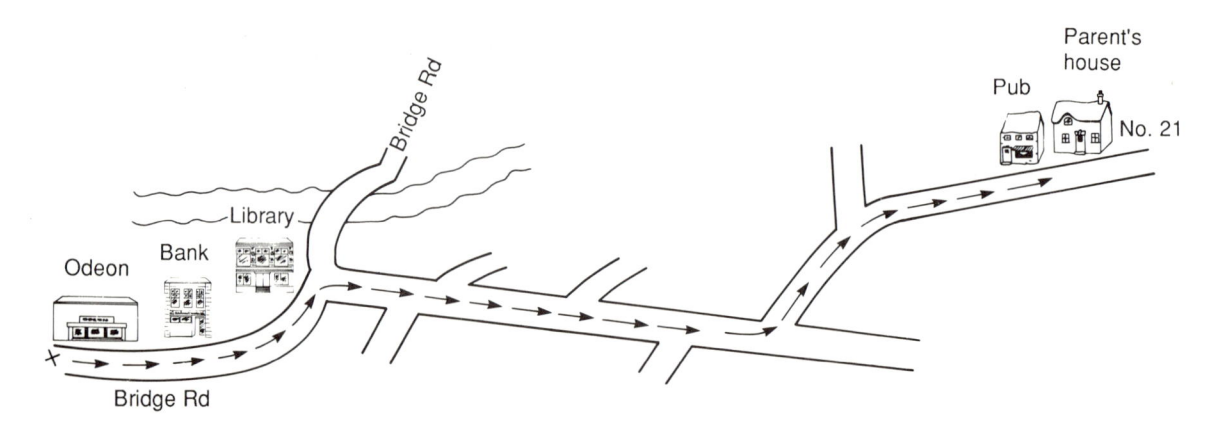

(a) I leave you this note / tell you how / get / my parents' house / Sunday.
Answer: I'm leaving you this note to tell you how to get to my parents' house on Sunday.

(b) It's best / come / bus but not forget / get / at the Odeon Cinema / Bridge Road.

(c) Go straight / Bridge Road / you get to the bridge, pass a bank / library / your way.

(d) Turn right just / the bridge and then take / on your left.

over the moon.
sick as a parrot

SPEECHES AND INSTRUCTIONS 37

(e) About 50m / on you have / bear right / fork.
(f) Carry / for another 100m and you see a pub / left; their house / first one / the pub.
(g) I / sure / not get lost so I wait / you at about 10.00.

B. Giving a speech at a wedding

You are the Best Man at the wedding of George and Margaret Burns. In Britain the Best Man – chosen by the bridegroom – has to pass the wedding rings to the bridegroom at the right time in the ceremony and usually makes a speech during the reception afterwards. You have been asked to make a short speech.

Here are the notes you have made. Complete the speech started below by expanding the notes.

Write it out

The Speech!

1. Get attention with joke! *Bride's parents*
   Thank Bridesmaids + especially the Burns – lovely reception etc.

2. Known George since schooldays
   Describe first meeting – broken bike – angry parents!
   Describe growing friendship.

3. Describe time at University with George and with Margaret in final year.

38 SPEECHES AND INSTRUCTIONS

> Tell the story of Margaret + George on holiday — car breaking down — George (Engineering student!) unable to do anything — Margaret fixing it — obviously useful person to marry!
>
> 4 Wish George + Margaret happiness, success etc etc. Finish with "So I'd like to finish by asking you to drink to the Bride and Groom."
>
> Excuse me, could I have your attention Ladies and Gentlemen? As the Best Man I shall make a short speech although I hope I won't keep you from your drinks too long! I'll start by thanking the lovely Bridesmaids for everything they've done today, and Mr & Mrs Burns for ---

C. Exam practice

Choose any of these titles and write a composition of between 120 and 180 words. Each composition should take no more than 45 minutes.

(a) A friend is staying in your flat while you are on holiday. Leave her instructions to look after your dog, find the things she'll need to cook with and turn off the water and electricity in an emergency. Also tell her where useful shops are and how to get to the city centre.

(b) Write instructions for a friend for a game or the use of a complicated machine – for example a video recorder, a camera or a dishwasher.

(c) You are the manager of a large hotel in a city in your country. Prepare a speech welcoming a group of Australian tourists and telling them about the hotel and the attractions of the city.

(d) It is your eighteenth birthday. Your family and friends have organised a surprise party for you. The meal has just finished and everyone is calling for you to make a speech. Write what you would say.

(e) You are a famous person in your country and have been invited back to your old school to talk to the pupils. Tell them about your experiences at the school – especially the ones you found useful in later life – and give them advice for the future.

UNIT 5 | Formal letters

finish

You will practise:
- organising the layout (addresses, date etc.) correctly
- planning and organising formal letters
- improving use of capital letters
- using suitable introductory and concluding sentences
- changing from informal to formal writing
- making a formal complaint using connecting words

Part 1 Planning and layout

Focus on the topic

What kind of person do you think the Grant Home is looking for? Think about sex, age, qualifications, experience, personal skills and qualities etc.

✸ **WELFARE ASSISTANT** ✸

needed at weekends to help with outings and leisure activities for mentally handicapped boys.

The Grant Home provides care and accommodation for handicapped boys.

More details and letters of application to:

Personnel Officer,
The Grant Home,
Vicarage Rd,
Birmingham B17 3TS

We are an Equal Opportunities Employer

40 FORMAL LETTERS

A.1 Here is a list of paragraph headings for a letter of application for this job. Put them in the order you think is best.

(a) A meeting/contact in future
(b) Reason for writing
(c) Personal skills and interests relevant to job
(d) Qualifications and work experience

2 Now read the letter of application and answer the questions.

---

16 Maners Way,
Aston,
Birmingham B19 6XP
24th March 1989

Dear Sir/Madam,

I am writing to apply for the post of Welfare Assistant recently advertised in the Daily Record.

I am twenty-two years old and left school in 1984 with three 'A' levels. At present I am in my third year of a degree course in Social Administration at Birmingham University. I have been working on a voluntary basis one afternoon a week for the last six months at the Work Experience Unit in Birmingham for physically handicapped youngsters.

I enjoy playing a wide variety of sports and very much like working with children. The fact that my younger brother is severely paralysed has given me a keen insight into, and interest in, the development of handicapped people. Therefore I feel that the job you are seeking to fill would be very rewarding on the personal level and would also give me useful work experience closely related to my field of study.

I can be contacted at the address above (tel. 269378) and would be available for interview at your convenience.

Yours faithfully,
Nora Mellors
Ms Nora Mellors

FORMAL LETTERS 41

(a) Has Nora got a good chance of getting the job? Why?
(b) Put the paragraph headings in Section A1 into the order they appear in Nora's letter and compare this order with yours.

B. Read the reply to Nora's letter and answer the questions below.

> The Grant Home
> Vicarage Road
> Birmingham
> B17 3TS
>
> March 28 1989
>
> Ms N Mellors
> 16 Maners Way
> Aston
> Birmingham B19 6XP
>
> Dear Ms Mellors,
>
> Thank you for your letter of 24th March.
>
> I read your application with interest and invite you to attend an interview at 2.30pm on Thursday April 6th at the Grant Home. Could you please confirm your availability for interview by telephone (369241 ext. 9)?
>
> I look forward to meeting you.
>
> Yours sincerely,
>
> *Jane Davenport*
>
> Jane Davenport
> Personnel Officer

1 (a) Why does Jane Davenport's letter include the recipient's (receiver's) address while Nora's letter does not?
   (b) Would it be wrong for Nora's letter to include the recipient's address?
   (c) The address on the left includes the recipient's name but the sender does not put her own name above her address on the right. Would it be wrong for the sender to type in her name above the address?

2 One letter is written by hand and the other typed; because of this there are two differences in layout between the letters. What are they?
   (a) Punctuation
   (b) Paragraphing

Note: It is not wrong to paragraph and punctuate a typed letter like a handwritten one. However, a handwritten letter should always be fully

FORMAL LETTERS

punctuated and the first line of each paragraph indented (started a short way in from the margin) like Nora's.

C. Formal letters usually have a structure like this:

First paragraph: introduction
Middle paragraph(s): main contents
Final paragraph: conclusion

Here are three groups of ideas for things to include in each of the main parts of a formal letter. Match each group with the part of the letter (introduction, main contents or conclusion) that it gives ideas for.

Group 1
(a) looking forward to some contact with the reader in the future
(b) thanking the reader for their interest/help
(c) offering to help/give information in the future

Group 2
(a) giving/asking for information
(b) making a complaint
(c) arranging a meeting

Group 3
(a) thanking reader for letter
(b) referring to an earlier telephone call, meeting etc.
(c) if it's the first letter, referring to the way you found out about the reader (advertisement etc.)
(d) giving reasons for writing/general idea of rest of letter

Which of these ideas did Jane use?

There is a composition on this subject at the end of the unit

Part 2 Practice of language points

A.1 Punctuation – capital letters

Change small letters into capitals where necessary.
(a) ms. p. g. yates,
7 hart road,
west bromley,
kent br1 1nh
(b) dear roger,
many thanks for the hospitality your company showed us on wednesday june 2nd.
(c) i would say that doctor smith is the best english doctor i know.
(d) last year christmas day was on a thursday.
(e) tim is studying maths; his ambition is to be the most famous mathematician in scotland.

FORMAL LETTERS 43

2 What types of word in the exercise above start with capital letters?
Examples: A person's title (Ms); initials (P. G.); a person's name.

B. Opening and closing phrases – the salutation and valediction

You are writing formal letters to the people below. This information is all that you know about these people. Write the correct opening and closing phrases.

People	Opening salutation	Closing valediction
manageress, female	Dear Madam	Yours faithfully
Paul Freen	Dear Mr. Freen,	Yours sincerely.
Jane Griggs, single *(Ms)*	Dear Miss Griggs,	sincerely.
sales manager, male	Dear Sir	Yours faithfully.
Elizabeth Parks *(Ms)*	Dear Ms. Parks	Yours sincerely.
teacher	Dear Sir/Madam	faithfully.
T. L. Smith, married, female *(Mr)*	Dear Mrs Smith	Yours sincerely

C. Style – formality

Decide if each of the phrases and characteristics in this list would be best in a personal or a formal letter.

	Phrases/characteristics	Type of letter
1	'Dear Madam'	formal
2	'Dear Mr Peters'	formal
3	'My dear Alex'	informal
4	'How are things, then?'	informal
5	'Thank you for your letter of ...'	formal
6	'See you soon'	informal
7	'Please do not hesitate to contact us if ...'	F
8	'Yours faithfully'	F

44 FORMAL LETTERS

9	'Yours'	In
10	'Love'	In
11	address of both receiver and sender	F
12	no contractions ('I'm,' – 'I am')	F
13	less social communication	F
14	full name under signature	F

2 A friend of yours has written this letter. Although there are no grammar mistakes, there are some mistakes in the layout and it is far too informal.
   Rewrite the letter by:
   (a) correcting the layout.
   (b) leaving out three unnecessary sentences.
   (c) making the rest more formal.

~~Will Brain,~~
16 George Street,
Wigtown,

Mr Paul Dangerfield,
Bradford College,
Bradford,
~~Yorkshire~~

Dear Mr ~~Paul~~ Dangerfield,

~~We haven't met before but I hope things are well with you.~~ I saw your advert in the local paper the other day so I'm writing for info. about your evening computer classes. ~~They sound pretty good really!~~ I would be grateful if you could send me detail*s* of these classes and also include the cost.
~~Anyway, send me the course details if it's not too much trouble (and the cost of course!)
Yes, I think I should enjoy these classes. Hope to get all these things from you fairly soon, then.~~

I look forward to hearing from you soon.

Yours ~~faithfully~~ sincerely,
~~Will Brain~~
~~(Mr Will Brain)~~ W. Brain (Mr)

FORMAL LETTERS

D. Introductory sentences

These sentences are common ways of starting the body of a formal letter. Write one word only in each space. Where there is a verb in brackets before the space, you may need to change the form of the verb.

Example: It was a _____ meeting you and (hear) _____ your ideas on education yesterday.

Answer: It was a pleasure meeting you and hearing your ideas on education yesterday.

(a) I am (write) *ting* to (inform) *inform* you *about* the arrangements for next week.

(b) Your company has been (recommend) *ed* to me *by* a friend and I am interested *in* (find) *ting* out more about your products.

(c) I am thinking *of* (go) *going* *on* holiday to Spain and was (wonder) *ing* whether you *could* send me some information about the North.

(d) Thank you *for* your letter *of / dated* May 1st (enquire) *ing* about my book.

(e) With *reference* to our telephone conversation, I can (confirm) *→* the time we provisionally (agree) *agreed* upon.

E. Concluding sentences

These sentences are common ways of ending the body of a formal letter. Complete the sentences in the same way as in Section D.

(a) I look *forward to* (hear) *hearing* from you in the *near* future.

(b) (Hope) *ing* that this information will be of *use* to you.

(c) It has been a *pleasure* (do) *doing* business with you.

(d) Please *do* not (hesitate) *→* to contact me *if / should* you need any *further* assistance.

(e) *Once* again, *may* I say *how* grateful we are for your very generous gift.

Part 3 Guided writing

Planning a letter of complaint

You have just returned to your own country from a very unsatisfactory four-week English course in England.

A.1 Imagine some of the problems you had, both in and outside school. Explain these to other students.

46 FORMAL LETTERS

2 This is part of the school's brochure which helped persuade you to go in the first place. Below it are your notes about what the school was actually like. Underline the parts that say the opposite of your notes.

The School

The Speakeasy School of English is in a quiet residential neighbourhood of Oxford but only a short bus ride away from the city centre and the famous colleges. There is easy access to the railway station and major bus routes.

Teaching

All the teachers are highly qualified and have at least three years experience of teaching English as a Foreign Language (EFL). Our carefully designed classrooms are pleasant places to work in and fully equipped. You can enjoy the benefits of learning through the use of videos, computers and a language laboratory. We offer special classes for all the important international EFL examinations (such as Cambridge First Certificate) and pronunciation classes for particular nationality classes. For all other classes the school sets a limit on the number of students from any particular country so that no group has a majority of students of one nationality.

Accommodation and Social Activities

The School can arrange for students to live with English families. Special care is taken over individual dietary requirements. We arrange our own extensive social and sports programme, making full use of our many facilities. Activities include trips to famous cities, theatre visits, football matches, film evenings and our popular disco-parties! We encourage students to meet English people as much as is possible and to get to know the local

Your notes:
- very noisy, close to railway station
- no classes offered for v. important American TOEFL exam
- no blackboard, proper desks; 'classroom' was actually a storeroom
- 70% of students my nationality
- all social and sports activities in city centre 4km away
- teaching, accommodation with family fine

FORMAL LETTERS 47

3. Complete the table using notes rather than full sentences from the brochure.

Original statements in brochure	Surprising, conflicting facts
	noisy – railway station
	no TOEFL classes
	classroom a storeroom
	70% my nationality
	sports, social events 4km away

4. You can make a complaint more effective by using 'although', 'despite' or 'in spite of' to make the difference and conflict between facts stronger.
   Make these notes into complete sentences by adding words and changing the form of the words in brackets if necessary. The first one has been done for you.
   (a) Although / brochure / (say) / school / quiet / I (find) / very noisy
       Answer: Although the brochure says the school is quiet, I found it very noisy.
   (b) Despite / brochure / (say) / school / quiet / neighbourhood / in fact / noisy because / near / station
   (c) Although it (state) / school / quiet / reality / noisy
   (d) In spite of your (say) / school / quiet / in actual fact there / lot noise

Now make similar sentences with a partner about the other four complaints.

B. Writing a letter of complaint

Back at home the rest of your family has advised you to write a letter of complaint to try to get some of your money back from the school. Write the letter using the plan below, not forgetting to include addresses etc.
Paragraph 1: Explain your connection with the school and when it was. Give your reason for writing – one sentence only.
Paragraph 2: Make your complaints – use 'although' and 'despite' once each.
Paragraph 3: Mention that school not all bad – give examples.

Paragraph 4: Say what you want the school to do now.
Paragraph 5: A suitable concluding sentence.

C. Exam Practice

Choose any of these titles and write a composition of between 120 and 180 words. Each composition should take no more than 45 minutes.
(a) Write to a hotel to book a room for three nights. Say what kind of room you want and the meals you require. Ask about sports facilities and local places of interest.

FORMAL LETTERS

(b) You want to go to an English school in London. Write to a school a friend has been to and ask about all the things you will need to know.

(c) Write a letter of application in response to an advertisement for a job you would like.

(d) You had a car accident recently. Your insurance company wants to know exactly what happened. Reply to them with a detailed description.

(e) You have bought an expensive camera which is now not working. Write to the makers describing the problem and suggesting a solution.

DESCRIPTIONS 49

UNIT 6 — Descriptions

You will practise:
- planning and organising descriptions
- punctuation – apostrophes
- using words to express your attitude and feelings
- paragraphing for clarity and emphasis
- writing descriptions of people and places from notes and pictures

Part 1 Planning

Focus on the topic

In pairs describe the picture to each other.
- what country might it be? Why?
- describe the scenery and the buildings
- what kind of people might be on the ship?
- why are they on the ship? What kind of journey might they be on?
- Tell your partner about a boat trip you have been on.

[handwritten annotations: life raft; life belt / buoys; In the foreground. sailing along; in a distance; they've; on a cruise; sea-sickness; on a ~~cruise~~ cruise]

50 DESCRIPTIONS

A. Read the text and answer the question below.

Text 1

Corfu Town

Corfu Town (or *Kerkyra* in Greek) is the capital of the green and fertile island of Corfu. It has a population of about 30,000 and lies on the east coast of the island protected by a ring of distant mountains.

The livelihood of the town is based on the tourist industry and trade in the agricultural products that come from the rest of the island. There is a busy port that sees a regular coming and going of both passenger and cargo ships.

The buildings of the town exhibit the strong influence of Corfu's Greek, Italian and British past. The old Venetian quarter is of particular interest to the tourist; one can spend many pleasant hours wandering through the narrow streets past high balconied buildings, old churches and the occasional palace or theatre.

As one might expect in a town with many tourists, you are never far away from a bar or discothèque. In the more traditional *tavernas* you may find Greeks dancing *Sirtaki* – a sad and lonely performance that is a means of self-expression for each dancer. It is rude to applaud but visitors almost always do and the Corfiotes will – of course – excuse your ignorance!

Read the list and choose the four subjects which are the most accurate headings for the paragraphs in Text 1. Put them in the same order as the paragraphs they describe.

Entertainment 4   People
History   Transport
Food and drink   Architecture 3
Economy 2   Geography 1

B Read Text 2, ignoring the words you do not understand, and answer the questions below. This is a description of the arrival of a traveller by ship at the Greek island of Corfu. It is daybreak and the sun is rising above the hills of Albania which lie behind the ship.

Text 2

That rosy old satin dawn, sending its warm pencils of light through the ravines of the hills towards the islands is really and truly 'rosy-fingered'.

It is at this early point that the traveller begins to recognize the distinctive form and signature of things Greek. As the vessel *bowls* softly across the smiling bay, he sees the famous town coming up at him with its small screen of decorative islands. The journey has not taken as long as he thought – they will dock slightly before seven o'clock, and climb up on to romantic quays lined with as yet empty cafes, where yawning *douaniers* await them with their maddening questions. There is a string of moth-eaten *fiacres* lined up and waiting for him, with their horses wearing characteristic straw hats that are pierced to let the ears of the animals pass through. Hats which give them a rather drunken appearance.

But the beauty of the little town! He has been warned that he will not find a prettier in Greece and as time goes on this will become more and more evident. At the moment his only ambition is to step ashore and into

DESCRIPTIONS 51

(strong castle) one of those carnival *fiacres* which will draw him through the old Venetian *(fortress)* into the town of Corfu – where, doubtless, rosy-fingered waiters will be waiting to *(ply)* him with breakfast. (Adapted from 'The Greek Islands' by Lawrence Durrell) *(generously supply)*

1 Why is it difficult to think of short paragraph headings (as for Text 1) that give us a good idea of what the writer is saying?

2 Compare the two texts and decide which text each sentence describes best. The first one has been done for you.

   (a) It's more factual: it's full of information. *Answer:* Text 1
   (b) It's taken from a fairly neutral Tourist Guide to Corfu. 2
   (c) It's full of very expressive words and phrases: it's rather poetic in style. 2
   (d) It's taken from a very personal description of Corfu. 1
   (e) It's easier to understand. 1
   (f) It concentrates on the atmosphere of the place and the writer's feelings towards it. 2

3 Discuss, giving reasons:
   (a) which text you enjoyed reading more.
   (b) which type of description you would find more difficult to write.

C. More *factual* descriptions usually have three main parts:

   First paragraph: introduction
   Middle paragraph(s): development of the description
      (Usually the writer only starts a new paragraph when he or she moves onto a different aspect of the subject/title, e.g. from the economy of Corfu to its architecture.)
   Final paragraph: conclusion

1 Here are two groups of ideas for things to include in the introduction and conclusion. Decide which group gives ideas for the introduction and which for the conclusion.

   Group 1
      (a) a more 'colourful' or humorous aspect of the subject/title
      (b) a more personal comment on, or opinion of, the subject/title   *Conclusion*
      (c) how the subject/title may change in the future

   Group 2
      (a) some very general points about the subject/title
      (b) the writer's personal connection with the subject/title   *introduction*
      (c) the writer's main reason for choosing this subject/title

52 DESCRIPTIONS

2   In pairs, describe to each other your country or a town in your country in a fairly factual way. Use the following topics to give you ideas to talk about if you wish:

geography   population   climate   economy   history
architecture   tourist sites   entertainment   food and drink
people   what you like and dislike about it

There is a composition on this subject at the end of the unit.

Part 2 Practice of language points

A.1 Punctuation – Apostrophe (')

Apostrophes are used to show where a letter(s) or number is missing and for one other purpose. Read the paragraph below and note down:

(a) what the other purpose of the apostrophe is.
(b) which letters are missing (if any).
(c) when you use an apostrophe at the end of a word.

There's something up with James' cat. It's the third time it's refused food this week and Caroline's cat hasn't ever done that. I don't think we'd better give it any more of John's New Year's Eve party cake, otherwise '89 might be its last year! By the way, have you seen the cats' drinking bowls?

2   Rewrite these sentences putting in apostrophes where necessary.

(a) I wont write to Tonys son again if he doesnt write soon.
(b) These boys books arent the neatest books Ive ever seen.
(c) Man didnt walk on the moon until 69.
(d) Shes a great believer in womens rights.
(e) Its time the car had its service.

B. Attitude words

It's useful to use certain words to express your feelings/attitude towards things you are writing about.

1   Rewrite the sentences with the most suitable attitude word from those given below, using each word only once. The first one has been done for you.
What extra meaning does each attitude word give to its sentence?

naturally   actually   unfortunately   strangely enough
undoubtedly

(a) No, he's not really a friend. Actually I can't stand him!
(b) She's not very intelligent but _____ she always does well in exams.
(c) The accident wasn't my fault so _____ I refused to pay for the repairs.

(d) Pele was a great footballer; he was _____ the best goal scorer of his time.

(e) _____ I won't be able to come to your party on Saturday.

2 Read the following description and choose the best attitude word below to fill each gap.

Michael Jackson

He's been singing since he was seven and he still manages to sound as fresh and as different as ever. With love songs like 'Got to be there' and 'Ain't no sunshine', the exciting 'Billie Jean' (from the twenty-five million selling album 'Thriller') and 'Bad', I (1) _____ think Michael Jackson is a genius.

(2) _____, his being in the music business for so long – it's over twenty years now – has led to much gossip about Michael's private life. Accounts vary from his having a face lift to a sex change. Then there are the stories of his relationships with his animals. (3) _____, he does have a llama, a boa constrictor called 'Muscles' and his song 'Ben' is all about a young man's relationship with his pet rat. Michael has said (4) _____ that he loves rats, feels they are his friends and wanted to write a song about those feelings. I (5) _____ like this song as it expresses Michael's thoughts on friendship, loyalty and love so beautifully.

What I admire most about Michael Jackson is the fact that he seems so unassuming about his success, and (6) _____ it is his secure and loving family background that has helped him remain so level-headed. (7) _____ he wouldn't have achieved what he has without his incredible talent, and in my opinion he will go on to do even bigger and better things. I (8) _____ hope so anyway.

1 (a) personally (b) indeed (c) generally
2 (a) Surprisingly (b) Normally (c) Naturally
3 (a) Honestly (b) Admittedly (c) Truthfully
4 (a) openly (b) clearly (c) obviously
5 (a) indeed (b) particularly (c) completely
6 (a) strangely enough (b) personally (c) undoubtedly
7 (a) In fact (b) Of course (c) Really
8 (a) finally (b) certainly (c) absolutely

C. Vocabulary – describing feelings and impressions

All these words can be put in the sentence 'It is a(n) _____ city'.

terrifying   enchanting   depressing
magical   picturesque   lifeless
filthy   frightening   sad
elegant   graceful   sordid
dull   peaceful   attractive
relaxing

1 Decide whether each word gives a good or bad impression of the place.
Example: terrifying – bad impression

2 Now divide the list into eight pairs of words by matching each word with the one that is closest to it in meaning.
Example: terrifying, frightening

54 DESCRIPTIONS

D.1 Style – using paragraphing for clarity and emphasis

Look at the two pictures of what many people think are typical English and Australian men – stereotypes.

Discuss:
(a) Do you think that many Engish and Australian men look like this?
(b) What are your ideas of a 'typical' Australian and English person?

2 Read the description below by an Englishman visiting Australia. The paragraph breaks have been left out.
   Decide where the paragraph breaks should be in order to separate and emphasise the important parts of the description as shown here:

Paragraph 1: Short introduction – the writer's intention
Paragraph 2: Seeing the male and female stereotypes
Paragraph 3: Trying (unsuccessfully) to photograph these stereotypes
Paragraph 4: Conclusion – what he learned from the experience

I came ashore determined to forget all the jokes and cartoons and ridiculous stereotypes and to learn about Australia afresh. It was not easy. I looked around me with the freshest eye I could manage, yet I immediately noticed men wandering about in singlets and shorts, their muscles looking remarkably like sausages. I saw big, brazen women going about the streets dressed and made up for the stage, apparently in the belief that the best way to catch a man was to incite him to passionate attack. I saw some men, still in their youth, with the largest beer bellies it was possible to imagine, cultivated at great expense, and I was overcome by the noise people made and the difficulty they had in showing each other affection. Then, one day, I set out to photograph these things I had noticed. Not one revolting beer belly came my way; not one girl was dressed in such tasteless extravagance as to be worth photographing. To my annoyance I saw men and women appearing to be softly appreciative of each other. The truth came to me that I had been seeing only extremes in the crowd; the most flamboyant, the most threatening, just as an Australian in London would see only Poms dressed in pin-striped suits and bowler hats. The vast majority of Australians weren't like these stereotypes and I wondered how a few examples of extreme behaviour could so stamp and characterize a whole society.
(Adapted from *Jupiter's Travels* by Ted Simon)

3 Discuss:
(a) Do other people have a stereotype of men and women from your country? Does it give an accurate picture of the appearance and characteristics of your nationality?
(b) Many people think that all national stereotypes are false and very unfair. Do you agree? Why (not)?

There is a composition on this subject at the end of the unit.

Part 3 Guided writing

A.1 Descriptions of people

Work in pairs for the following speaking activity:

Student A
Look at the picture on page 56. Describe the picture and include comments on all the physical characteristics listed below. Do not show your picture to student B.

Student B
Keep your book closed and have a piece of paper and pencil ready. Listen to Student A's description and draw what you hear.

Compare pictures only when Student B has finished drawing.

Physical characteristics:
    face shape, complexion, eyes, nose, hair, scar, facial hair, facial expression; height, build, clothes

56 DESCRIPTIONS

2 All students write a single paragraph describing the picture below, including comments on all the physical characteristics listed above. Use suitable vocabulary to make your descriptions as expressive as possible.

shutter

B.1 Descriptions of places

Work in pairs as for Section A, question 1, but this time Student A has the book shut while Student B looks at the picture of a small town on p. 58.

Student B describes the scenery, buildings and activities going on in the picture; Student A makes a rough drawing. Compare pictures only when you have finished.

2   All students write a description of the town on p. 58. You are sitting at a table outside the cafe and writing the description in your diary. Use the following notes to help you.

   Paragraph 1: 'I'm sitting outside a cafe in the main square...'
   – what's the name of the town?
   – what's the weather like?
   – describe the scenery behind the town
   Paragraph 2: Describe the buildings.
   Paragraph 3: Describe what's happening around you.
   Paragraph 4: Describe your personal feelings about the town.

C. Exam practice

Choose any of these titles and write a composition of between 120 and 180 words. Each composition should take no more than 45 minutes.

(a) Describe the appearance, character and lifestyle of a typical person from your country.
(b) Write a description of the town or area of the country where you live to give information to tourists.
(c) Describe the room in your house that you feel most at home and relaxed in, and explain why.
(d) Describe a place you have visited that has made a strong impression on you; concentrate on the atmosphere of the place and your feelings for it.
(e) Describe your favourite season of the year and the effect it has on you and your country.

58 DESCRIPTIONS

ADVANTAGES AND DISADVANTAGES 59

UNIT 7 | Advantages and disadvantages

You will practise:
- planning and organising this type of composition
- linking ideas using punctuation and connecting words
- avoiding repetition of language
- making the other side of the argument weaker
- writing suitable introductions and conclusions
- writing a composition from notes

Part 1 Planning

Focus on the topic

Give the name of each form of transport in the pictures and discuss:
- Which pictures do you associate with which particular countries?
- What kind of journey is each used for? *Example*: A bus is usually used for fairly short (cheap!) journeys if you haven't got a car or if it's difficult to park.
- Which have you used? Tell another student about a good or bad experience you have had while using one of these forms of transport.

A. Read the composition and answer the questions below.

In the last fifty years flying has become the most popular form of international travel. However, there are both positive and negative points associated with it.

The most important advantage of air travel is that it is quick; you can fly from London to New York on Concorde in three and a half hours. Furthermore, travelling by plane is very easy; someone takes your luggage after you have checked in and all you have to do is get on and sit down.

60 ADVANTAGES AND DISADVANTAGES

You will have reserved a seat and a friendly air hostess will look after your every need. On long flights there are films and music to entertain you. Another point in favour of air travel is that it is now relatively cheap, especially for long distance travel. You can fly from London to Sydney for £600 whereas by ship it can cost £2,000.

On the other hand, travelling by air has its disadvantages. Perhaps the most obvious is the element of danger involved. However, despite the publicity given to hijackings and crashes, flying is in fact one of the safest forms of transport. Undoubtedly the traveller misses out on seeing places on the way to his or her destination; obviously flying over the Pyramids is not the same as climbing them! In addition to these points, long distance air passengers can get very tired and mentally and physically confused by time changes – many precious days of holiday may be wasted recovering from jet lag.

To conclude, although flying involves inconvenience and slight risk, I would say that the advantages outlined above outweigh the disadvantages.

1 Think of a suitable title for the composition.

2 Here are possible headings for each of the four paragraphs of the composition. Put the headings in the order in which they occur in the composition.
(a) Advantages
(b) Writer's overall opinion
(c) Historical overview
(d) Disadvantages

B. Now complete the plan the writer used for this composition, noticing how the 'spider plans' for paragraphs 2 and 3 show the main points and their examples clearly.

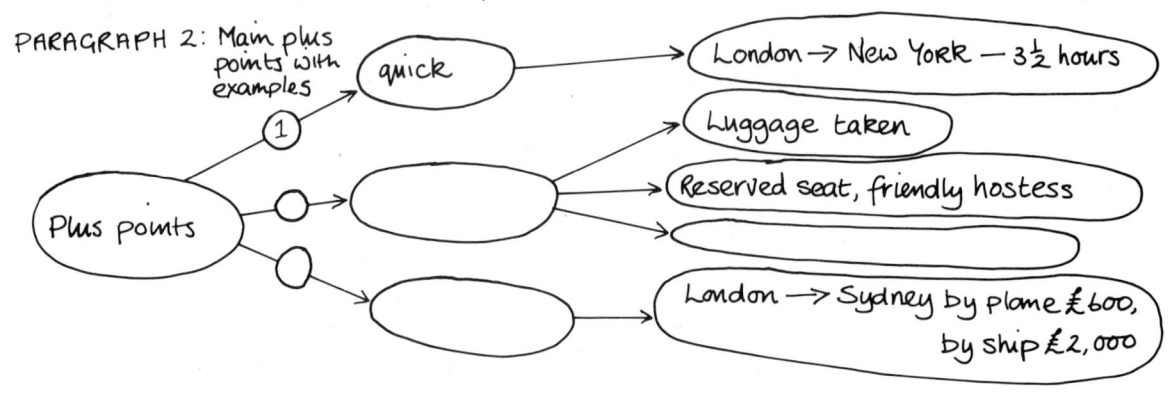

PARAGRAPH 1: Most popular form of transport now, but are both plus and minus points.

PARAGRAPH 2: Main plus points with examples

- Plus points
  - ① quick
    - London → New York — 3½ hours
  - Luggage taken
  - Reserved seat, friendly hostess
  - London → Sydney by plane £600, by ship £2,000

PARAGRAPH 3: Main minus points with examples

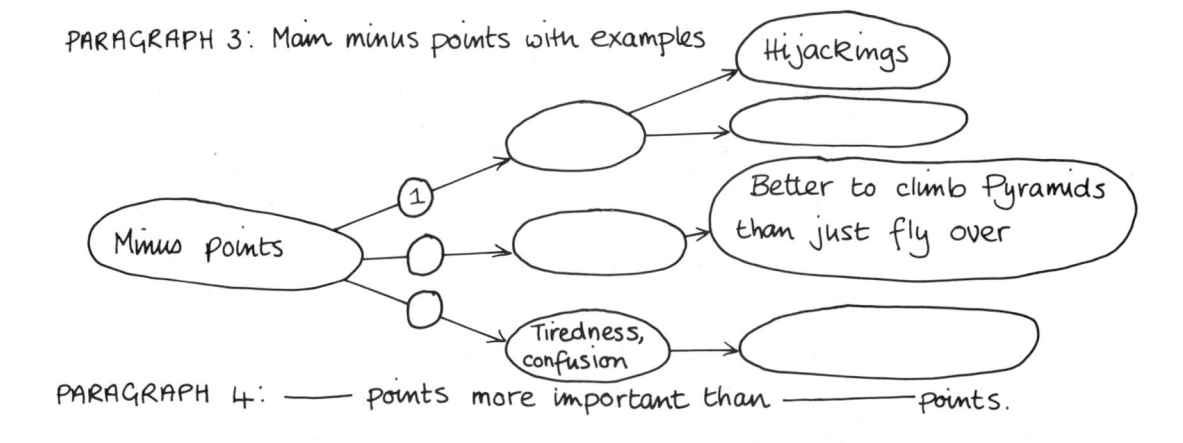

[Diagram: Minus Points branching to three sub-nodes (1, and two others), leading to examples: Hijackings; Better to climb Pyramids than just fly over; Tiredness, confusion; and other empty bubbles]

PARAGRAPH 4: ——— points more important than ——— points.

C. 'Advantages and disadvantages' compositions often have a structure like this:

    Paragraph 1: introduction
    Paragraph 2: advantages (or disadvantages)
    Paragraph 3: disadvantages (or advantages)
    Paragraph 4: conclusion

Here are four groups of ideas for things to include in each of the main parts of an 'advantages and disadvantages' composition.

Match each group with the part of the composition (introduction, advantages, disadvantages or conclusion) that it describes.

Group 1:
    (a) the positive points
    (b) examples of these points

Group 2:
    (a) your overall opinion – but don't repeat anything you've already said
    (b) summarising the most important positive and negative points
    (c) weighing up the positive and negative points
    (d) imagining how the subject will change in the future

Group 3:
    (a) the negative points
    (b) examples of these points

Group 4:
    (a) your interest in the subject
    (b) your general opinion about the subject
    (c) an historical overview of the subject
    (d) why so many people disagree about this subject

Note: The ideas for things to include in introductions are very similar to those for introductions to 'opinion' compositions.

Part 2 Practice of language points

A.1 Punctuation – semicolon

Read these sentences and decide if it is possible to use full stops or commas in place of the semicolons, and explain why.

(a) Travelling by plane is very easy; someone takes your luggage and all you have to do is find your seat and sit down.
(b) Air travel is quick; you can fly from London to New York on Concorde in three and a half hours.
(c) The air traveller misses out on seeing places on the way to his destination; obviously flying over the Pyramids is not the same as climbing them!

2 Complete these sentences with a comma or a semicolon.

(a) Gas is perhaps the most common fuel for heating__ it is also just about the cheapest.
(b) Many people commute from Hertford to London by car__ while others use public transport.
(c) Peter finished his work just before six__ he had hoped to finish earlier.
(d) Computers are a common feature of today's classroom__ in my day they were unheard of.
(e) He owns three paintings by Constable__ one of Britain's greatest artists.
(f) Mary seems to think she'll get the job__ I don't think she's got a chance.

B. Connecting words

This exercise revises the connecting words introduced in Part 2 of Units 1 and Part 3 of Unit 5.

Fill each space with the most suitable of the connecting words given below.

Recently I watched a programme on television which claimed it had the answer to improving your memory. (1) _____ it also said it had a simple but effective method of learning new vocabulary in a very short time. I was more interested in the latter part (2) _____ I'm learning Arabic; (3) _____ I've already forgotten the first bit on general memory improvement! Anyway, the basic idea is to associate a picture in your mind with the word you want to learn.

Imagine you want to learn the Arabic word for tea, which is 'shai'. First think of a word in English – (4) _____ whatever your first language is – which reminds you of 'shai'. I thought of the English word 'shy' as it has a similar sound to 'shai'. (5) _____ done this, you then fix a picture in your mind which combines the word in your language with the meaning of the Arabic word 'shai', and concentrate on this picture for a few seconds before going on to the next word. So I concentrated hard on a mental picture of a group of shy people drinking tea in silence. And I really did remember the word and its meaning!

You may think this is an extremely silly way to learn vocabulary.
(6) _____ there is no doubt in my mind that it really works. (7) _____ this method seems to help many people remember new vocabulary for long periods of time.

(8) _____ I don't think this method would work so well for advanced learners because it is more difficult to think of vivid pictures for difficult, abstract words. (9) _____ it would be easy to confuse the pronunciation of the word you're learning with that of the similar sounding word in your language.

(10) _____ this method is not the only way to learn vocabulary, I would still say that it is an effective technique for many people. Anyway, why don't you try it and see if it works for you?

1 (a) However (b) Moreover (c) Although
2 (a) and (b) due to (c) as
3 (a) because (b) then (c) in fact
4 (a) if (b) or (c) but
5 (a) When (b) After (c) Having
6 (a) However (b) Despite (c) Although
7 (a) Another point is that (b) So (c) But
8 (a) Also (b) What is more (c) On the other hand
9 (a) What is more (b) So (c) But
10 (a) However (b) Although (c) Because

C.1 Making the other side of the argument weaker

Read the following paragraph. Is it more likely that the writer agrees or disagrees with the idea that television is harmful for children? How do you know?

> It has been said that watching television is harmful for children. Some people argue that it discourages children from being active and developing their minds and bodies. I have even heard the argument that watching cartoons encourages children to be violent towards each other! However,...

2 Imagine that there is a plan to ban all lorries and private cars from the centre of your nearest city: only bicycles and buses are to be allowed.

(a) Think of three points that support the plan, and three that are against it. Here are some ideas to help you: pollution, traffic/parking problems, difficulty for local shops, inconvenience for visitors with cars.
(b) Decide if you agree with the plan or not, and find another student who disagrees with you.
(c) Discuss the plan with the other student, using some of the following phrases to introduce and weaken the points which you don't agree with.
   It has been argued/said that... but/however I feel that...
   Some people say/argue...
   It could possibly be said/argued that...
   I have (even) heard the argument that...

There is a composition on this subject at the end of the unit.

64 ADVANTAGES AND DISADVANTAGES

D. The concluding paragraph

The following sentences are all taken from concluding paragraphs. Replace the underlined words with the words given in brackets, changing other parts of the sentence if necessary. The meaning of the whole sentence should stay the same.

Example: There is no doubt that the disadvantages <u>outweigh</u> the advantages. (important)
Answer: There is no doubt that the disadvantages are more important than the advantages.

(a) <u>In short</u>, we have seen that heavy government spending may cut unemployment, but will probably lead to inflation. (sum up)
(b) <u>Weighing up both sides of the argument</u>, I feel that nuclear weapons will do more harm than good in the long run. (balance)
(c) It is clear that <u>on the whole</u> television does less harm than good. (general)
(d) There is no doubt that the <u>major</u> factor in the argument is the one of health. (important)
(e) <u>To conclude</u>, the advantages of your idea make our acceptance of it absolutely necessary. (conclusion)

E.1 Style – avoiding repetition

What is wrong with using the underlined words in the paragraph below?

2 Replace each underlined word or phrase with a different word which has the same meaning.

John is a salesman. (a) <u>John</u> likes his job although sometimes (b) <u>his job</u> is rather boring. Two or three times a year his (c) <u>job</u> takes him outside Britain as his company often gets contracts (d) <u>outside Britain</u>. John is (e) <u>often</u> asked to go to Scotland; this suits him as (f) <u>Scotland</u> is where his family come from so he never goes too long without seeing (g) <u>his family</u>.

Part 3 Guided writing

A.1 Introductory paragraphs

Here are four introductory paragraphs for the composition title, 'The Prison System Does More Harm Than Good'. Discuss. Of course we need to see the complete compositions to assess the introductions fully. However, two are clearly less suitable than the others; decide which and why.

(a) Most people in prison in my country have been sent there because they have committed some kind of theft, although there are, of course, many murderers etc. Theft is becoming increasingly common, especially where credit cards and jewellery are involved.
(b) It is easy to find fault with the prison system. However, we should not forget that every civilised society in the world has used imprisonment

ADVANTAGES AND DISADVANTAGES

66 ADVANTAGES AND DISADVANTAGES

   as the major way of dealing with crime. Without it civilised life as we know it would not be possible.
   (c) Prisons certainly provide work for a lot of people and help some prisoners to learn skills useful for work. A lot of convicts benefit from the time prison allows them to think about themselves and their lives.
   (d) In a discussion about a topic as important as the prison system it is essential to look at both sides of the argument. I shall, therefore, examine both the advantages and disadvantages before presenting my conclusion.

2 Looking at the two preferred paragraphs, can we get any idea of whether the writers are for or against the prison system?

B.1 Organising your ideas – from notes to composition

Here are some notes about prison. Work with two or three other students and decide which opinions support the prison system (pros), and which oppose it (cons). The first two have been done for you. Add some ideas of your own.

> (a) very expensive (con)
> (b) keeps dangerous people away from normal society. (pro)
> (c) makes it very hard for prisoners to readjust to normal life when they get out.
> (d) doesn't help convicts to become better people.
> (e) discourages people from committing crimes.
> (f) creates jobs — prison warders, cleaners etc.
> (g) most criminals commit more crimes when they get out.
> (h) is an inhuman way to treat human beings.
> (i) puts criminals in the company of other criminals only.
> (j) gives food, protection and security to people who often can't look after themselves.
> (k) is merely answering violence with violence.
> (l) gives criminals time to think about and sort out their lives.

2 Put the pros in order of importance. Now do the same for the cons.

3 You are going to write a composition of about 200 words entitled: '"The Prison System Does More Harm Than Good." Discuss.' First you need to cut out the pros and cons you think are not relevant or important. Avoid repetition. You will probably not need more than five or six different points altogether.

4 Draw up a simple plan; use the ideas in Part 1, Section C if you wish. You should be absolutely sure of your opinion on the subject by this stage.

5 Now write your composition; write an introduction different from those given in Section A(1).

C. Exam practice

Choose any of the following titles and write between 120 and 180 words. You should take a maximum of 45 minutes for each.

(a) In many countries young people have to do a period of military service. Do you think this is a good thing?
(b) Discuss the ways in which the motor car has changed our lives.
(c) What are the advantages and disadvantages of being an only child?
(d) 'Lorries and private cars should be banned from the centre of every big city.' Discuss.
(e) 'Watching television is a waste of time.' Discuss.

UNIT 8 Reviews

You will practise:
- planning book reviews
- punctuation – commas and full stops
- using connecting words to link reasons and results
- creating dramatic effect in your writing
- being clear and concise
- guiding writing of reviews
- set book compositions

Part 1 Planning

Focus on the topic

Match each book title with the type of book it is an example of. Then decide whether each is fiction or non-fiction.

Animal Farm   Cookery book
My Life and Times   Text book
Encyclopedia Britannica   Play
A Basic Science Course   Biography
The Life of Gandhi   Horror stories
Macbeth   Atlas
The World in Maps   Autobiography
100 Greek Recipes   Novel – fiction
'The Dead are Alive!' and other tales   Reference book

Which types do you read mainly for pleasure and which for information? Which of these types of book do you read a lot? Why?

A. Read this composition about one aspect of the novel *The Go-Between* by L. P. Hartley and answer the questions below.

> Though a simple story of a summer holiday spent at a friend's home, the book has as its main theme the ending of a young boy's innocence by the 'evil' of adults.
>
> Leo, the young boy, arrives at his rich friend's house, Brandham Hall, for the summer. Socially inferior, he finds the ways and manners of the people living there difficult but he makes friends with Marion, the eldest daughter. His love for her enables her to use Leo to send messages to her lover Ted. Leo innocently believes that the messages are purely business and is happy to act as a go-between. He is deeply shocked when he reads part of an unsealed letter from Marion to Ted and realises <u>they</u> are in love. He becomes even more caught up in the triangle when he learns that Marion is engaged to Lord Trimingham, someone she does not love. <u>His</u> loyalty to

Marion is severely tested as she still asks him to take messages between her and Ted. He cannot understand <u>this</u> as he believes that Marion should now love Trimingham. However, he takes a last message from Ted asking Marion to meet him. Believing he can break Ted's spell over Marion he tells her a different time and that night he also tries to make his own spell, which does not succeed. The next day, Leo's birthday, Marion's mother is convinced that Leo knows something about Marion and <u>she</u> drags him to a hut <u>where</u> the two lovers are discovered. <u>This</u> is the final shock from <u>which</u> Leo never fully recovers.

The result of this sad story is that Leo is so affected by the behaviour of the adults at Brandham that he is never able to love. At the age of fifty he returns to Brandham, meets Marion and once more feels the influence over him of the events of nearly forty years earlier. He has now become a sad and lonely man whose feelings of guilt and shame have destroyed his faith in other people.

1 Choose the best title for this composition:

(a) A description of the three main characters.
(b) How Ted and Marion fell in love.
(c) The effect on Leo's life of the events at Brandham.
(d) Leo's role in the love affair between Ted and Marion.

2 Complete the rough plan for this composition by writing one word in each space. The first letters of some of the words have already been written in.

Introduction: main _____
Middle paragraph: main e_____ of the story that influence L_____
Conclusion: e_____ on the life and character of _____

3 There are seven underlined words in the text. They all refer to words that come before them, either in the same sentence or the previous one. Write out the underlined words and the words they refer to.
Example: 'they' refers to Marion and Ted.

B. For a set book composition you may be asked to do one or more of the following:

– describe an important character
– describe or explain a part of the story
– tell part of the story as if you were one of the characters
– discuss one of the themes
– give your opinion about a character, a theme or the book as a whole

Working in pairs, think of a book or a film you have enjoyed recently. Describe to your partner:

– the outline of the story.
– one of the main characters or an important theme.
– why you particularly enjoyed it.

There is a composition on this subject at the end of the unit.

Part 2 Practice of language points

A.1 Punctuation – commas and full stops

Notice the different punctuation that the underlined connecting words take. Which punctuation marks could be left out? Which punctuation mark could replace the full stop before 'However'?

(a) She's generous and usually great fun to be with, <u>but</u> can be rather aggressive.
(b) She's generous and usually great fun to be with. <u>However</u>, she can be rather aggressive.
(c) She's generous and usually great fun to be with, <u>yet</u> can be rather aggressive.

2 Rewrite the following sentences adding commas and full stops (followed by a capital letter) where necessary.

(a) His writing is stylish and witty furthermore he never loses the attention of his readers.
(b) Scotland is very beautiful although it has an awful lot of rain.
(c) Elizabeth Taylor is the actress who married Richard Burton twice.
(d) Ronald Reagan who had once been an actor was one of the oldest American Presidents.
(e) You can enter the church free of charge however you are asked to pay 50 pence if you wish to take photographs.

B.1 Connecting words – talking about reasons and results

The following underlined words connect reasons with results. Decide which part of the sentence is the reason and which is the result. Which underlined words are more formal? The first one has been done for you.

(a) <u>The rains did not come</u>; <u>consequently</u> <u>there was even less to eat in 1987.</u>
      reason   formal   result
(b) I had to take a taxi <u>as</u> the bus didn't come.
(c) He was found guilty of murder and <u>therefore</u> was sent to prison.
(d) Our prices have risen <u>due</u> to an increase in the cost of materials.
(e) The shops were shut <u>so</u> I couldn't get any bread.
(f) <u>Owing</u> to the bad weather, there will be no trains today.

2 Join the sentences below using the words in brackets, paying particular attention to meaning, punctuation and grammar. You may have to change the order and wording of the original sentences. The first one has been done for you.

(a) The Head teacher asked her to leave the school. She was always rude to her teachers. (therefore)
Answer: She was always rude to her teachers; therefore the Head Teacher asked her to leave the school.
(b) The book was very exciting. I enjoyed it very much. (as)

(c) He wrote a brilliant composition. He got good marks in the exam. (owing to)
(d) There has been a strike by delivery men. There are no newspapers today. (consequently)
(e) I've tied a knot in my handkerchief. I won't forget to phone you. (because of)
(f) You'd better take my umbrella. It's raining. (since)
(g) She went to see the film again. She had really enjoyed it the first time. (so)
(h) There have been improvements in health care. People live longer now. (due to)

C. Style – being clear and concise

Read this extract from a book review which needs to have some changes made and answer the questions below.

> The main character (perhaps the most important person in the book,) is Peter Straw. He's a tall, powerfully built (strong) man whose mental and emotional toughness reflects his physical strength. (Because of his strength) he has little difficulty dealing with the fights in the bar he runs, and his inner strength seems to stop him getting hurt in any of the many relationships he has with women. That is until Diana comes along. (His relationship with her is different.)
>
> Diana has tremendous self confidence and belief in herself. She doesn't run after Peter and this not chasing after him seems to attract him. Eventually after a while they become friends but soon Peter realizes that for the first time he needs a woman more than she needs him. This has never happened before. He sees this as a weakness and from this point on his life changes.

1 The writer is going to leave out of the first paragraph the words she has put in brackets. Why did she choose those words?

2 Make the second paragraph more concise by choosing to leave out:
(a) one complete sentence
(b) three parts of different sentences

D.1 Inversion

Look at these two sentences. Which one has a more dramatic effect?

(a) He <u>had</u> <u>never</u> <u>been</u> so frightened; he <u>never</u> <u>travelled</u> by plane again.
(b) <u>Never</u> <u>had</u> <u>he</u> <u>been</u> so frightened; <u>never</u> <u>did</u> <u>he</u> <u>travel</u> by plane again.

2 Look at the underlined parts of the sentences again. Complete these notes describing the ways in which sentence (b) is different from (a). Choose a word from the following to fill each space:

did   first   replaced   between

(a) The 'inverting' word (Never) comes _____ .
(b) The subject (he) comes _____ the auxiliary (had) and the main verb (been).

(c) If there is no auxiliary, then the main verb (travelled) is _____ by the correct auxiliary (_____) and the infinitive (travel).

Note: This inversion of the subject and the auxiliary is often used for dramatic effect, for example when describing a story or your reaction to a story, and will help you to demonstrate a wide range of expression in your writing.

3 Now rewrite the following sentences using the 'inverting' words in brackets. Remember that the 'inverting' word starts the sentence. The first one has been done for you.

(a) Her perfume was so overpowering that he had to leave the room. (So)
Answer: So overpowering was her perfume that he had to leave the room.
(b) I've never laughed so much in all my life! (Never)
(c) They had just sat down outside in the garden when it began to rain. (Hardly)
(d) I've rarely seen such a beautiful film. (Rarely)
(e) I didn't know at the time that the book was going to change my life. (Little)
(f) Sting writes fantastic songs. He sings well, too. (Not only...but he also...)

Part 3 Guided writing

A.1 Film reviews

Read the information about the people and then look at the film reviews. Decide which films would be the most suitable for each person or pair of people.

Lucy, aged 20.
Is studying French at university. Enjoys serious films but not any with violence in them.

Bernie and Sue, aged 25.
Sue loves frightening films and can't stand love stories. She is also interested in factual films. Bernie hates horror films and enjoys love stories. He is interested in history.

Jim, aged 35 and daughter Sarah, 10
Recently divorced from his wife. Both enjoy light films that are full of adventure, especially where the unexpected happens.

Film Certificate Categories:

'U' No age limit.
'PG' No age limit although parents/guardians should know that the film contains material they might prefer children under 14 not to see.
'15' Only suitable for person of 15 years or over.
'18' Only suitable for persons 18 and over.

REVIEWS 73

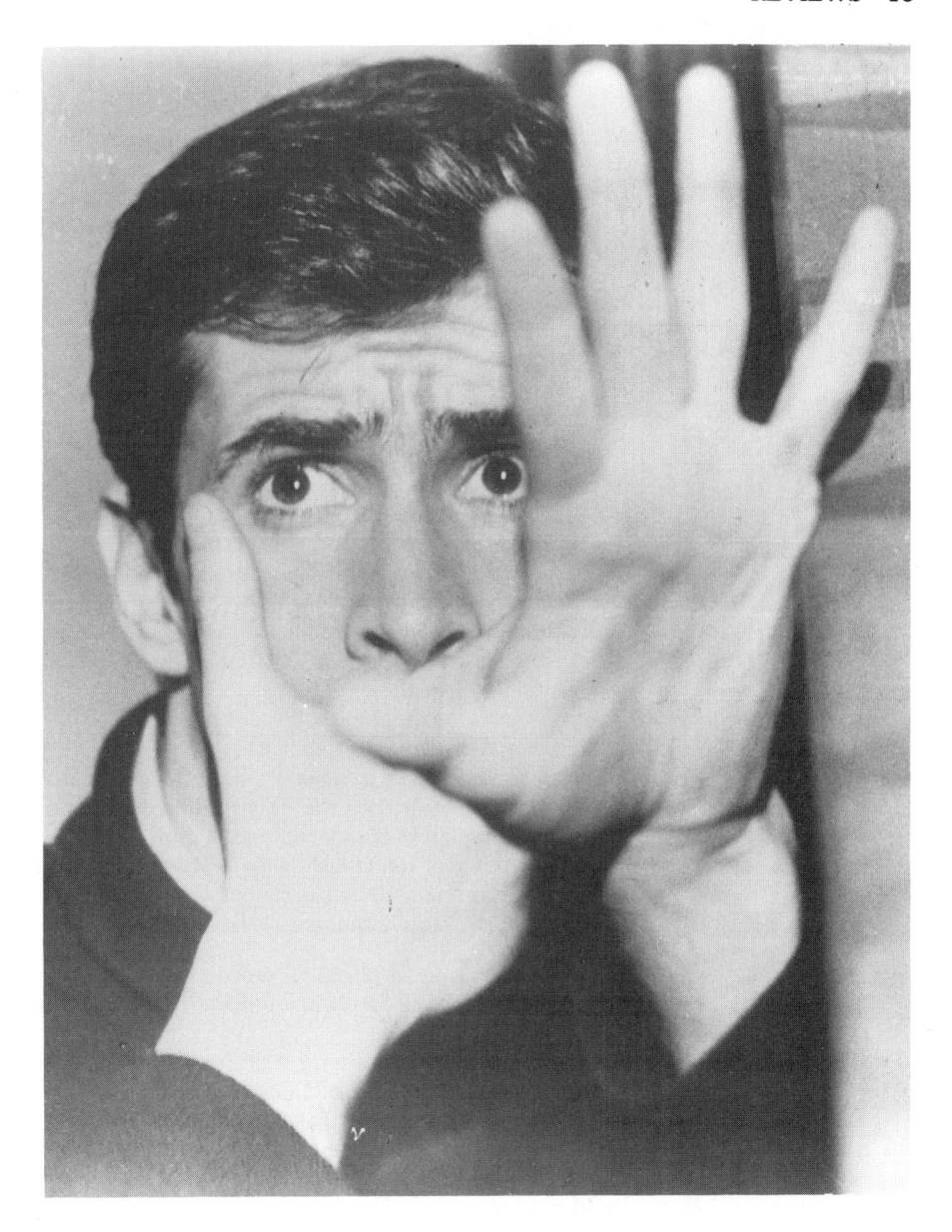

Psycho (18)
A secretary steals a large amount of money from her office. Driving through the pouring rain she stops at a lonely motel. Although the receptionist seems a bit strange she thinks nothing of it and takes a room. What happens next will have you screaming in your seats. A film for the strong willed!

REVIEWS

The Last Emperor (15)
A true story based on the life of Pu Yi who became emperor at the age of three but died many years later in Peking as a humble gardener. As the story unfolds, we see Pu Yi growing up, treated like a god until he is expelled to Tientsin where he lives as a local ruler. When the communists take over China, Pu Yi changes his attitude and becomes a gardener for the rest of his life. A film worth seeing if you want to learn about the modern history of China.

Jean de Florette (PG)
Jean Cadoret lives on a farm in Provence. The Soubeyrams, who want his land, stop up the water that feeds Jean's crops. However, due to his farming skills the crops do well until the summer when there is no rain. This film shows how the seasons dictate people's lives and their behaviour towards each other. A moving film which will make you cry. Don't worry about the language; there are English subtitles.

Star Wars (U)
The beautiful Princess Leia is captured by foreign forces and it seems her country will fall into ruin. However, the charming hero, Luke, sets out to recapture the Galactic Empire and stop these evil forces. He also has the help of his friendly robots. An action packed film for everyone who likes adventure in space.

Kramer v Kramer (15)
Joanna Kramer walks out, leaving her husband to look after their young son. At first Mr Kramer finds the daily routine difficult but gradually we see how their relationship deepens into one of trust and love. When Joanna comes back for her son, the father fights for custody in the courts and loses. However, Joanna realises she cannot take her son away from her husband. A moving portrayal of father–son relationship.

2 Write a paragraph of about 50 words for each of your three choices of film, giving clear reasons for your choices. Begin the paragraphs as follows:

Paragraph 1: I recommend that Bernie and Sue should see . . .
Paragraph 2: The best choice for Jim and Sarah would be . . .
Paragraph 3: I suggest that Lucy should go to . . .

B.1 Reviewing the words of a song

Read the title of this Beatles song without reading the rest of the song. Imagine what the song might be about.

She's leaving home

Wednesday morning at five o'clock as the day begins
Silently closing the bedroom door
Leaving the note that she hoped would say more
She goes downstairs to the kitchen clutching her handkerchief
Quietly turning the backdoor key
Stepping outside she is free

She's leaving home
'We gave her most of our lives'
'Sacrificed most of our lives'
'We gave her everything money could buy'
She's leaving home after living alone for so many years, bye bye

Father snores as his wife gets into her dressing gown
Picks up the letter that's lying there
Standing alone at the top of the stairs
She breaks down and cries to her husband, 'Daddy our baby's gone.'
'Why would she treat us so thoughtlessly?'
'How could she do this to me?'

She's leaving home
'We never thought of ourselves'
'Never a thought for ourselves'
'We struggled hard all our lives to get by'
She's leaving home after living alone for so many years, bye bye

Friday morning at nine o'clock she is far away
Waiting to keep the appointment she made
Meeting a man from the motor trade

She's having fun
'What did we do that was wrong?'
'We didn't know it was wrong'
Fun is the one thing that money can't buy
Something inside that was always denied for so many years, bye bye
She's leaving home, bye bye

© 1967 Northern Songs Ltd. Reproduced by permission of EMI Music Publishing Ltd and International Music Publications. Photocopying of this copyright material is illegal.

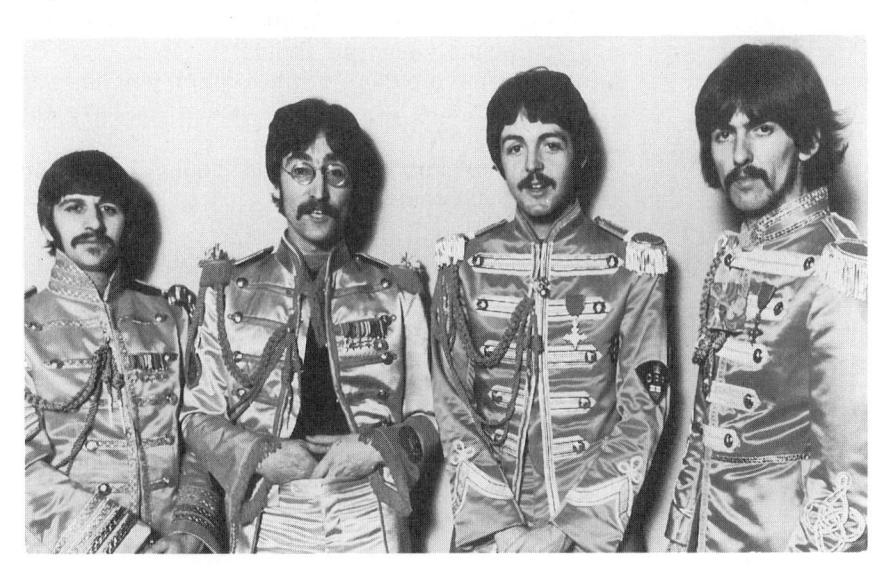

2   Which one of the following is the main theme of the song?

(a) Falling in love
(b) Problems between parents and children
(c) Moving house

3   Discuss:

(a) Who are the four people mentioned in the song and what are the relationships between them?
(b) Why did the girl leave home?
(c) The parents' words are in 'speech marks'. Do the parents think that the bad relationship is their fault or their daughter's?
(d) Is the song writer more sympathetic to the parents or the daughter? Give reasons.
(e) What attitudes and behaviour – on either side – can lead to a teenager running away from home in your country?

4   Write a report on the song using the following notes:

Paragraph 1: Describe the main theme and single main event of the story.
Paragraph 2: Explain why the girl left home.
Paragraph 3: Say whether you think the writer is more sympathetic to the girl or her parents and explain why.
Paragraph 4: Describe one thing that you particularly like or dislike about the song.

C. Exam practice

Choose any of these titles and write a composition of between 120 and 180 words. Each composition should take no more than 45 minutes.

(a) Describe a character and his/her influence on the story in a book, play or film you have read or seen recently.
(b) Describe the main events of a book, play or film and explain what you particularly enjoyed about it.
(c) Describe a picture or photograph you like and your feelings about it.
(d) Explain how a book, play or film you have enjoyed deals with its main theme.
(e) Tell the story of a particular book, play or film as if you were one of the main characters.

UNIT 9 Checking and correcting compositions

You will practise:
- assessing, correcting and improving compositions
- some spelling rules

Part 1 A letter

A. Teachers sometimes use symbols to help you correct mistakes you have made in your writing. The thick lines show words or parts of words that need correcting and the symbols show what kind of mistake has been made.

1 Study this list of correction symbols and then correct the mistakes in the sentences below. The first one has been done for you.

```
A      —  a mistake with the article ('a', 'the')
w/o    —  the word order is wrong
vb     —  the wrong verb form
prep   —  the wrong preposition
gr     —  a grammar mistake (other than the ones above)
voc    —  the meaning is wrong (the wrong word)
sp     —  a spelling mistake
∧      —  a word is missing
p      —  a punctuation mistake
n/c    —  not clear, needs rewriting
sty    —  the style or level of formality is wrong
```

                                                           hadn't seen

(a) vb She wishes she <u>didn't see</u> him yesterday.
(b) w/o They asked why <u>didn't I</u> want any tea.
(c) gr, ∧, p I'm very <u>interesting</u> in playing a game ∧ football on <u>tuesday</u>.
(d) vb I'll see you when you <u>will come</u>.
(e) gr, prep, gr There were <u>such</u> many things to do while I was <u>in</u> holidays.
(f) voc, ∧ I must <u>remember</u> my friend to go to ∧ dentist.
(g) sp, gr I'm <u>studing</u> <u>this</u> books because I have to <u>make</u> an exam
    voc tomorrow.

78 CHECKING AND CORRECTING COMPOSITIONS

2. The letter below was written by a student in reply to a letter from a friend. The friend's letter is on page 18. Correct the mistakes (wherever there are words underlined) using the correction symbols to help you. Some have already been done for you.

---

12 Tweedale,
Cherry Hinton,
Cambridge,
England.

22th April 1988

← Dear Peter,

Thanks a lot for your letter. It was really great to hear from you. Our friends at hospital are getting on very well. They always ask about you. The last
vb three weeks at the hospital <u>weren't</u> very exciting, but it seems that we will have <u>many</u> (a lot of) patients ~~the~~ next month. Hard work!

As you've heard I got married and
gr, vb (in four month) I <u>expect</u> a baby. I'm <u>shure</u>
sp that I'll give up my job after the birth of my little child. My husband, Henry, works in
gr <u>a</u> insurance - company.
vb I would really <u>looking forward</u> (like) to visiting you in Australia with my family, but at
sty the moment I am too busy. ∧∧∧∧....

Well, once more, thank you very much for your lovely letter and all the best (for the future) ~~wishes~~!

Love, Kim

CHECKING AND CORRECTING COMPOSITIONS 79

B. These corrections help improve grammar, vocabulary, spelling and punctuation. However, they don't improve the overall organisation and meaning of the letter.

Complete these comments about the letter by putting one word in each space.

Organisation and layout:

> The words "____ ____" should be further over to the left. Although it isn't wrong as it is, it would be more natural to put "____" directly under "Love".
> Other than this the layout is very good.
> The organisation into paragraphs is excellent.
> It would be more natural to explain ____ you are too ____ to visit Australia (paragraph 3)

Range of language used:

> The language used is suitably informal. However, the range of vocabulary used is not very ____. Similarly, the grammatical structures used are all fairly ____.
> Good, appropriate use of punctuation.

Grade for First Certificate (A, B, C or Fail): _____

Part 2 A narrative

A. This composition was written by a student practising for the First Certificate examination. The title of the composition is 'A horrifying experience'.

1 Correct the mistakes using the symbols to help you. Some have already been done for you.

80 CHECKING AND CORRECTING COMPOSITIONS

> It happened during my stay in Cambridge. I was with some friends at Roch's pub drinking a beer. Suddenly we heard a loud crash coming from the road.
>
> We ran out and saw a car *had* smashed into the side of a large petrol tanker. The car had probably shot out of the junction without seeing the tanker coming. The driver of the car died instantly, the passenger in the car and the tanker driver were both severely injured. But shortly after the injured people had been taken to the **sp** _ospital the junction became a fireball.
>
> What had happened was that the tanker *was carrying* contained petrol and started leaking out and **vb,sp,p** spread all over the road. The _ as usual, **voc** some careless passer stopped and threw a cigarette down in the road. You can imagine what happened. It was a miracle no one else was injured.

2   Read the composition again and answer the following questions. Discuss your answers with a partner.

(a) Does the composition match the title? Are there any irrelevant parts?
(b) Is the division into paragraphs acceptable? What is the subject of each paragraph?
(c) Is the story easy to follow?
(d) Are there many mistakes? Which of them are simple, basic ones?
(e) Does the writer use a wide range of grammar and vocabulary? Make a note of words or phrases in the composition that you rarely or never use.
(f) What grade would this composition get in First Certificate (A, B, C or Fail)?

B. Spelling in English is a big problem! However, there are some rules that are very useful and quite easy to learn.

CHECKING AND CORRECTING COMPOSITIONS

1 (a) Complete this list showing how the spelling of words ending in 'y' changes.

    Verbs   try ⟶ tries   buy ⟶ buys
    (present tense):   study ⟶ _____   pay ⟶ _____

    Plurals: party ⟶ parties   holiday ⟶ _____
         family ⟶ _____   boy ⟶ boys

    Comparative   lucky ⟶ _____   grey ⟶ greyer
    adjectives: happy ⟶ happier   gay ⟶ _____

    Superlative   dry ⟶ driest   coy ⟶ coyest
    adjectives: funny ⟶ _____   grey ⟶ _____

(b) Now complete the rule for all words ending in 'y' in the four categories above. Put one word in each space.

If the letter before the 'y' is a_____, change the 'y' to 'i'.
If the letter before the 'y' is a_____, do not change the 'y'.

(c) Complete the following rule in the same way.

When you add an 'ing' ending to a word which ends in 'y' you always _____ the 'y'. So 'pay' becomes 'paying' and 'study' 'studying'.

2 (a) Complete the table and note when a consonant is doubled in the middle of a word.

    Verbs: stop ⟶ stopped ⟶ stopping
         beg ⟶ begged ⟶ _____

         cool ⟶ cooled ⟶ cooling
         peel ⟶ _____ ⟶ peeling

         dine ⟶ dined ⟶ dining
         hate ⟶ hated ⟶ _____

    Adjectives: flat ⟶ flatter ⟶ flattest
         thin ⟶ _____ ⟶ thinnest

         mean ⟶ meaner ⟶ meanest
         poor ⟶ poorer ⟶ _____

         fine ⟶ finer ⟶ finest
         pale ⟶ _____ ⟶ palest

(b) Complete this rule about the doubling of consonants. Put one word in each space.

When you add an ending to a word you only double the consonant if the original word ends in a single _____ and has a single short _____ before that consonant.

82 CHECKING AND CORRECTING COMPOSITIONS

However, as with most rules in English, there are exceptions!
- Many longer words, e.g. benefit ⟶ benefiting.
- Some irregular verbs (if the pronunciation of the vowel changes from long to short), e.g. bite ⟶ bitten.
- x and y are never doubled.

Part 3 A discursive composition

A. Read this composition, which was written by a student practising for the First Certificate examination, and answer the questions below. When you have finished discuss your answers with a partner.

"The prison system does more harm than good: discuss."

        gr   Nowaday many crimes are commited like every day and
        sp   many criminals are sent to ∅ prison. Ordinaly people
        Vb, ʌ   think that the criminals have to go to ∅ prison is ʌ natural
        w/o   affair. But why ⌃the criminals should go to prison?
                Because they should be punished by law and in addition
                to give them time to think about their lives. However
        vb p   the criminals don't realize how stupid ʌ things ʌ they did,
        n/c ʌ   perhaps they will be back again someday. It's ʌ waste of
                money.
                It is important to keep dangerous people away from
                normal society and to keep them under ∅ surveillance.
        ʌ, vb   If they weren't sent ʌ prison, we are worried about our
        vb   life. On the other hand, ʌ to make it very difficult for
                prisoners to readjust to normal life when they get out.
        gr, ʌ   They can't find a job easier, neither can get ʌ trust of
        p   other people. These problems are not only prisoners' their
        ʌ   families, particulary ʌ children, are gotten hardship of
              n/c   their own life.
        gr   It's difficult to say that the prison system is
        n/c   good or not good. It will be different from a situation.
        sty   anyway it's difficult for ∅ man to judge a man.

(a) Organisation of ideas:
- Why is the first paragraph not a good introduction? Which three sentences should be in a later paragraph?
- How many ideas are there that support the prison system and how many that are against it? Are these ideas arranged in a logical order into appropriate paragraphs?
- Does the conclusion clearly explain the writer's opinion about the topic? What is her opinion?

(b) Accuracy of language:
- Are there many mistakes? Give some examples of simple, basic mistakes.

(c) Range of language:
- Does the writer use a wide range of grammar and vocabulary? Make a note of words or phrases in the composition that you rarely or never use.

(d) Grade:
- What grade would this composition get in First Certificate (A, B, C or Fail)?

B. Rewrite this composition improving it as much as you can. Keep to the ideas of the original composition but:
- correct the mistakes indicated by underlining.
- make sure the ideas are clearly expressed.
- change the order of the ideas.
- divide the composition into suitable paragraphs.
- expand the conclusion to make the writer's opinion clear.